HANDSEL BOOKS
Montale in English

EUGENIO MONTALE (1896–1981) was born in Genoa and worked as a journalist and critic. He was an early opponent of Fascism and was deeply affected by his experience of the First World War and its aftermath. He was the leading poet of the modern Italian "Hermetic school," in which the suggestive and symbolic power of words is as important as their objective sense. His reputation was established by the intense lyrical vision of his first three collections of poetry: *Ossi di seppia* (1925, "Cuttlefish Bones"), *Le Occasioni* (1939, "The Occasions") and *La bufera e altro* (1956, "The Storm and Other Poems"). In *Satura* (1971) a new disillusioned voice emerged in Montale's poetry, commenting ironically on post-war Italian society and debunking his own previous poetic myths. He was awarded the Nobel Prize for Literature in 1975.

HARRY THOMAS is the translator of Joseph Brodsky's "Gorbunov and Gorchakov" (*To Urania*, Penguin, 1987) and the editor of *Selected Poems of Thomas Hardy* (Penguin, 1993) and *Talking With Poets* (Handsel Books, 2002), a collection of interviews with Robert Pinsky, Seamus Heaney, Philip Levine, Michael Hofmann, and David Ferry.

MONTALE IN ENGLISH

Edited by HARRY THOMAS

HANDSEL BOOKS

an imprint of
Other Press • New York

First published 2002, Penguin UK

Copyright © 2002, 2004 Harry Thomas

Production Editor: Robert D. Hack
Text design: Natalya Balvova
This book was set in Sabon by Alpha Graphics of Pittsfield, NH.

10 9 8 7 6 5 4 3 2 1

Library of Congress Cataloging-in-Publication Data

Montale, Eugenio, 1896-
   [Selections. English. 2005]
   Montale in English / edited by Harry Thomas.
       p. cm.
   Includes index.
   ISBN 1-59051-127-1 (pbk. : alk. paper)   1. Montale, Eugenio,
1896—Translations into English.   I. Thomas, Harry, 1952-   II. Title.
   PQ4829.O565A2 2005
   851'.912–dc22

                                                      2004019887

The acknowledgments on pp. 237–244 constitute an extension of this copyright page.

CONTENTS

Mediterraneo

LE OCCASIONI

Mottetti

LA BUFERA E ALTRO

SATURA

DIARIO DEL '71 E DEL '72

QUADERNO DEL QUATTRO ANNI

ALTRI VERSI E POESIE DISPERSE

HOMAGES TO MONTALE

PREFACE

This book brings together around one hundred of Montale's poems in translations by English, Scottish, American, Australian, and Italian translators. Before I began compiling it, I thought I had a good idea of the history and force of Montale's presence in English. But the more days I spent on the prowl in libraries, the more astonished I was to discover just how many English versions of Montale's poems have been made since 1927, the year that the first one, G. B. Angioletti's prose paraphrase of "Spesso il male di vivere ho incontrato," appeared in the *Criterion*. In the end I have decided to include the work of fifty-six translators, but I might have included that of dozens more. The one real regret I have, though, is the absence from this anthology of several translations – Henry Reed's rendering of the great "Mottetti," for instance – which repose unprintably in archives.

In selecting the translations, I have kept in mind the two standard criteria of the anthologist: interest – the need to let the reader see much of what there is to see – and interestingness – the need to stop readers in their tracks as often as one can by printing what is in one way or another genuinely good. Interest has meant for me two things. First, I have sought to represent the full range of Montale's poetry, drawing primarily on his first three books – *Ossi di seppia* (1925), *Le occasioni* (1939), and *La bufera e altro* (1956) – while not scanting the poems in *Satura* (1971) and the books that Montale wrote after it – *Diario del '71 e del '72* (1973), *Quaderno di quattro anni* (1977), and *Altri versi e poesie disperse* (1981). At times Montale spoke somewhat sceptically of these books. Once, he called them his *retrobottega*, goods from the back of the shop. Critics and translators, especially American ones, have inclined to dismiss them out of hand. I like a great many of the poems of this second Montale, and it is my hope that readers of the last quarter of this book will come to like them too.

Second, I have wanted to represent the range of kinds of poetic translation – metaphrase, paraphrase, and imitation – to use Dryden's still excellent terms. For a while, recalling that Robert Lowell remarked in his preface to *Imitations* that he sometimes preferred "modest photographic prose translations" to verse translations, and that Montale himself occasionally expressed the same preference, I flirted with the notion of reprinting some of the prose photographs in, for example, Stanley Burnshaw's *The Poem Itself*. Two prose translations do appear in this book, but now, with the permission of the translators, lineated. Finally, in an effort to help the reader to consider the methods and to calculate the merits and demerits of the various modes of translation, I have offered in the case of several poems the Italian original and two or more translations of it.

As for the second criterion: the first-rate translation, that miracle of renewed sense and reanimating form, which is still, like the original poem, bamboo-dry, is, of course, a rarity. It may be that no translation in this book performs the miracle. But I feel sure that a number of the translations come as close to the miraculous as we may have any decent right to expect, and that many can be read and reread with pleasure as English poems.

A word on the headnotes. In most instances, I have gone in for the laconic headnote – the translator's name, dates, important publications – or the critical headnote – this translation illustrates the following, etc. – or a combination of the two. Where I have felt that celebration or restoration is in order, I have given myself permission, as it were, to draw a personal sketch of the translator.

INTRODUCTION

In the Chronology in Jonathan Galassi's *Eugenio Montale: Collected Poems, 1920–1954*, the first half of the entry for 1967 reads: "June: Honorary degree from Cambridge University; named Senator for Life by President Giuseppe Saragat."[1] The phrasing of this, with its toneless severity, may seem to suggest for a moment that the relation between the two events in June was one of cause and effect: the Italian President, upon learning that Montale had been embraced by the great English university, rewarded him at once with the highest honor his country could bestow.

The entry is suggestive beyond the pleasing misreading. As G. Singh pointed out many years ago, Montale was the first major Italian poet to prefer English literature to French or German literature. He felt, in fact, an affinity for English, the English and a lot of things English. In "An English Gentleman," an amusing story in *Farfalla di Dinard*, his book of short stories (a book that, in his Preface to Singh's translation of it, Montale remarked he had managed to write only because he had a Ligurian sense of humor and was "a great admirer of the English essayists"), the narrator tells of his acquaintance with "a gentleman who spends his Christmas holidays in Switzerland where he practises a sport invented by him – that of the bogus Englishman." The narrator soon confesses that he has been trying to emulate the gentleman for years, and declares in the final sentence: "All I know is that in a hypothetical Association of Bogus Englishmen he ought to be made President and I Vice-President." Montale himself made many trips to England, a few on holiday. More than one of his Italian friends attributed his reticence at gatherings to "Englishness." During the twenty years he lived in Florence, he did so, he wrote in the Singh Preface, "in close contact with the English colony, which in those days was quite large."[2] Elsewhere, he said he had tried to live in Florence "like the Brownings."[3] From his late twenties, he occasionally signed his letters "Tiresias," in homage to *The Waste Land* and its author, and for some time in his thirties he and Mario Praz – Praz tells the story in his autobiography, *La Casa della vita* – "exchanged poems in a macaronic English which was a parody of the English of Pound's and Eliot's verses."[4]

That his poetry began to be known in England almost as soon as it had made him known in Italy delighted Montale. His fame in Italy came early, with the publication of his first book, *Ossi di seppia*, in 1925. From the moment the book appeared, as Henry Gifford has said, "Montale became the poet with most to say to contemporaries who would heed him."[5] It was, as it turned out, two Italians, Praz and G. B. Angioletti, who, in articles on contemporary Italian literature in the *Criterion* and the *London Mercury*, first brought Montale to the attention of English readers. Both men knew the Italian literary scene well, and in introducing Montale to the English they also communicated a feel for life on the ground in Italy. Angioletti wrote first in the *Criterion* (June 1927):

From Eugenio Montale, one of the few Italian "europeists," comes *Ossi di seppia*...a little book of lyrics which has aroused much interest among readers of taste for the originality of its intonation, its warm, passionate sense of Nature and for the felicity with which the young poet has succeeded in rendering concrete, in strongly realistic images, the most difficult and complicated states of mind.

Six months later, Praz, writing in English from Liverpool, where he was then a professor of English, concluded his column for the *London Mercury* (January 1928) with these sentences:

Eugenio Montale's (born in Genoa in 1896) (*Cuttle-bones*), first published in 1925 and now going through a second edition, fully deserves the name of poetry. Montale's verse has all the elusive magic of the Ligurian sea-coast, the infinite movement of those arid promontories washed by the surge of the changing sea. The Ligurian landscape is constantly suggested in these poems; the connexion between nature and soul could not be more intimate.

Soon after writing this encomium to his friend, Praz sent his English translation of "Arsenio," a poem Montale had published in a magazine just the previous summer, to another friend, T.S. Eliot, the editor of the *Criterion*. When Eliot printed the translation in that summer's issue (June 1928), Montale was overjoyed. In *La Casa della vita*, Praz recalls how Montale wrote to swear "eternal gratitude" to him: "I shall never forget. *Nevermore*."[6] (The next year, Montale returned half the favor by publishing translations of three of Eliot's *Ariel* poems.)

In 1932, Praz provided this giddy sketch of Montale for the *London Mercury*:

Be it summer or winter, one is sure every night to come across there ["at a cafe in the main square of Florence"] Eugenio Montale, the landmark in Italian poetry of the last decade, and librarian of the world-famous Gabinetto Vieusseux...[7]

Already by 1930, Montale's reputation in Italy was so high that an American, Samuel Putnam, the editor of the international magazine *This Quarter*, could write in an issue of that magazine devoted to new Italian literature:

Of the poets represented, Eugenio Montale is one of the best beloved of present-day Italian lyricists...The dominant note in Montale is a cosmic despair. He is a sort of modern and lyric Lucretius, who has read his Einstein, his Bergson, and others. His ideal remains, however, a pure lyricism.[8]

Montale was only thirty-three at the time and had published just one book.

When, in June 1934, *The Times Literary Supplement* ran a long article on modern Italian poetry, in which Montale was singled out as the poet who had made the "greatest impression" in Italy among the postwar poets and was said to have the closest affinity to Eliot, Montale's reputation in England seemed secured. Almost immediately, however, his reputation plummeted. As far as I know, his name appeared in print in England only once more before the late forties: Mario Praz, in his "Italian Chronicle" in the *Criterion* (January 1938), lit into Montale as a poet in whose work "Biedermeier ideals and moods are unmistakable." "Beidermeier" Praz defined as

a small world of common sense and healthy habits, delights of the home and cult for tamed and well-groomed Nature, observance of sound principles, minute love for the concrete, with, every now and then, a flight on the wings of a sweet, and often gently sad, dream...

What the critic had given, the critic had taken away.

Meanwhile, in Florence, in April 1933, Montale met the most important English-speaking person of his life, the young Dante scholar from New York, Irma Brandeis. The Montale and Brandeis story is one of the more intriguing romantic-literary stories of the last century, but most of the facts are still not known. What is known and worth recording here is the role that Brandeis played in introducing Montale's poetry to American readers. Her "Italian Letter" in the July 1936 issue of the *Saturday Review of Literature* was the first essay on Montale to appear in the United States, and included the first translations of his poems. Brandeis was a brilliant scholar-critic, but it is doubtful whether her essay won Montale many American readers. She had more success as his champion after the Second World War, first as the one who introduced his poetry to James Merrill, the best of the early translators, and then, in 1962, as the editor of the Montale issue of the *Quarterly Review of Literature*, the first anthology of Montale's poetry in English.

In the years just after the war, Montale began to be heard of again in England. To a significant extent, this was the doing of Bernard Wall. Wall edited at that time an important magazine, *Changing World*, and in it and other magazines he published his translations of several poems that Montale had written since the early thirties, including the first translation into English of "La casa dei doganieri," for which Montale had won a literary prize in Florence back in 1931. Wall also used *Changing World* to beat the drum for Montale, as he did in "From A European Notebook, 1948":

I left early for Milan – two and a half hours by express through the Appenines. S. met me at the station. I immediately rang up Montale and we dined at a trattoria with him and several of his friends ... Montale told me that he would like to live in London. I wish this would come to pass as the presence of an Italian literary figure is badly needed there ... But it is hard to see who would appreciate such an excellent writer as Montale, who in my opinion is one of the four or five best European poets now living. I know hardly any other Italian who has such a profound knowledge of English literature.[9]

Wall was not a poet, and he made no claims for his translations as poetry. He was that kind of translator who seeks to subordinate himself to the poem for the sake of the poet.

The watershed in the history of Montale in English was the publication in 1962 of Robert Lowell's *Imitations*. Lowell served as an index of his generation's interests, and when he published his translations of ten of Montale's poems, and said in the book's introduction that he had "long been amazed by Montale,"[10] many American and English readers discovered a new interest and source of amazement. Elizabeth Bishop, after first looking into *Imitations*, wrote to Lowell: "I went through it very rapidly and concentrated most on the Montales – I've never read him, or barely, and I'd love to."[11] That "I'd love to" is what a lot of readers have felt in the last forty years. One suspects that a good many of the translators in this book who were born after 1935 or so first read Montale in

Lowell's translations. Michael Hofmann said, in his review of Jeremy Reed's book of Montales, *The Coastguard's House*, that at this time "*Imitations* is more influential than any other aspect of Lowell's practice."[12] For many, not least of all Hofmann himself, who describes Lowell's versions as "so electrified and distorted by feedback their own mothers wouldn't recognize them,"[13] this is not a happy state of affairs. For some, however, Lowell has continued to serve not only as an introduction to Montale, but as a model for translating him. Jeremy Reed is one such:

it was through Lowell's brilliant imitations of Montale, poems which while remaining considerate to the original, take idiosyncratic liberties in language and the organization of the poem, that I conceived a way of bringing my own poetic drive and obsessions to a Montale poem, and somehow working up a collaborative fluency in place of a translation.[14]

It may be that *Imitations* liberated editors and publishers as well as poets and translators. In the decade after the publication of Lowell's ten Montales, two anthologies of Montales appeared in the United States: Glauco Cambon's *Selected Poems* (1965) and Brandeis's issue of the *Quarterly Review of Literature*. During the last thirty-five years, principally in translations by Charles Wright, G. Singh, William Arrowsmith, and Jonathan Galassi, Montale has become easily the best-known Italian poet in the English-speaking world. It was F. R. Leavis, not known for his passion for non-English literature, and not a reader of Italian, who, in his 1971 essay, "Eugenio Montale's 'Xenia,'" may have come closest to identifying the sources of Montale's power:

I will now hazard that, in a wholly unpejorative sense, Montale – it is an aspect of his unassertiveness – is as truly sophisticated as a major artist can be. The sophistication is apparent in the wit, irony and humour that intensify the effect of profound seriousness characterising his poetry. It is apparent in the way in which he conveys his sense of the supreme reality of Mosca. His delicate intensity of evocation makes us feel that, in a naive sense of "real," she is a real presence for us – that she is really "there."[15]

*

Montale's poems are notoriously hard to translate. Several of the translators in this book have gone on record saying so, and one suspects that those who have not recognize themselves in the confessions of those who have. The confessors have come up with a rather large lexicon for describing the poems: *difficult, obscure, hermetic* – we expect these; but also – *cryptic, riddling, slippery, private, closed-in, encoded, mysterious*, and *elusive*. Montale heard similar expressions of uncertainty and puzzlement from some Italian critics. That his response to them was usually irritated surprise, real or feigned or something in between, does not comfort the translator, who knows from experience that Montale is so hard that at times he appears to be impossible to translate well.

"No problem is as consubstantial to literature and its modest mystery," Borges observed, "as the one posed by translation."[16] A theoretical or categorical probing of the problem of translating Montale might prove illuminating, but I would prefer to look at length at one poem, "Verso Vienna," and the four translations of it – by Ben Belitt, Edith Farnsworth, William Arrowsmith, and Jonathan Galassi – that I knew as I put this anthology together. "Verso Vienna" appears in the first section of *Le occasioni*. It is not one of Montale's immortal poems. Only a few Italian critics have bothered with it, and among critics in English only Arshi Pipa, in his excellent book, *Montale and Dante*, has given it serious attention.[17] But the poem's inconspicuousness may allow us to see it more distinctly. The four translators are all fairly conservative in their approaches to the problem of translation. This, too, may work to our advantage. Although we may admire most the renderings of adaptors like Robert Lowell, Jeremy Reed, and Jamie McKendrick, we also know that they present several problems peculiar to themselves.

In October 1932, Montale made a trip by car to Germany and Austria. On October 10, he wrote to his friend Lucia Rodocanachi: "On my trip I've written to no one. Nuremberg is very tiresome but Vienna is lovely and the German women seem to me less ugly than I had expected."[18] The first draft of "Verso Vienna" dates from 1933, but Montale did not publish the poem until January, 1939, when, together with what, revised, became the sixth of the "Mottetti," it appeared in *La Gazetta del Popolo*, a Turin newspaper. Montale would seem to have revised the poem, perhaps fundamentally, between 1933 and 1939.

Verso Vienna

Il convento barocco
di schiuma e di biscotto
adombrava uno scorcio d'acque lente
e tavole imbandite, qua e la sparse
di foglie e zenzero.

Emerse un nuotatore, sgrondo sotto
una nube di moscerini
chiese del nostro viaggio,
parlo a lungo del suo d'oltre confine.

Addito il ponte in faccia che si passa
(informo) con un soldo di pedaggio.
Saluto con la mano, sprofondo,
fu la corrente stessa...
                            Ed al suo posto,
battistrada balzo da una rimessa
un bassotto festoso che latrava,

fraterna unica voce dentro l'afa.

Here, in the manner of the old Penguin series, I offer a plain prose translation:

Towards Vienna

The baroque convent of foam and biscuit shaded a shortened view of slow waters and set tables here and there strewn with leaves and ginger.

A swimmer surfaced, dripping under a cloud of midges, inquired of our journey, spoke at length of his own on the other side of the border.

He pointed to the bridge we faced, which is crossed (he informed us) for a penny toll. He waved farewell, went under, was the current itself ... And in his place, an outrider bounded out of a carriage house, a cheerful dachshund that barked,

a fraternal voice in the sultriness.

The poem is distinctly, if oddly, Dantesque. On a journey, the poet and his unnamed companion (or companions – the number is unspecified) arrive at a place on a river, a river they evidently intend to cross. A baroque convent looms above an outdoor restaurant on a cove. It is autumn: leaves lie strewn on the tables. (Or perhaps the leaves, *foglie*, are decoration. That ginger, in some form, fingers or sweetmeat, also lies "strewn" on the tables might seem to support this interpretation.) Suddenly, a swimmer surfaces in the water, in a cloud of insects. A conversation ensues, the swimmer speaking at some length of his journey, although exactly what he says or the poet says to him the poem does not say. The swimmer points to the bridge up ahead, informing the travelers that it costs a penny to cross it. Then the swimmer goes under, becoming one with the current. Taking the swimmer's place, a dachshund bounds out of a building (*una rimessa*), cheerful and barking. In a device that Montale liked, the poem ends with one arresting line set off from the rest of the poem.

The narrative, such as it is, seems clear enough, as do a majority of the details. A number of questions, though, will occur to the translator at once. What, for instance, is the relation between the setting of the opening stanza and the poet's encounter with the swimmer. Does the swimmer get out of the water or only surface in it? What is the border he has journeyed beyond, and how has he made the journey from there to here? By swimming? What, in this context, is the meaning of *battistrada*? Related to this last question is another: What kind of building does the dog come out of?

While the translator will need to ask these and other questions, and, if possible, answer them, the questions will have to be put aside for the time being, for what the translator needs first, in order to have any hope of finally making even an adequate translation, is a good grasp of the poem as a whole. The details can be rendered rightly only if the translator perceives the intention – by which I mean not the poet's intention, but what Umberto Eco has called the intention of the text – that informs and unifies them.[19] It is one thing to see that the *mise-en-scène* of "Verso Vienna" is Dantesque. To understand to what end it is this and how this end animates every detail – this is the translator's first, essential task. That it may also be the final task, and be one translators are never sure they have carried out well, however selfless and patient they have been in undertaking it, is what makes Montale so frustrating a poet to translate.

The part of a poem that may come closest to embodying, or at least to declaring, its unifying subject is, of course, the title. But "Verso Vienna" seems too formulaic a title to reveal much, if anything at all. *Verso* means both *towards* and *near*. "Verso" plus a place name is a formula Montale liked for his titles: "Verso Capua," "Verso Siena," "Verso Finisterre," and "Verso Lodi." On the face of it at least, "Verso" in a title would appear to be lexically stable. Whatever the word signifies in one title, whatever prepositional gesture it makes, it will signify the same thing and make the same gesture in every title. Jonathan Galassi, who is the only translator to have translated all of these poems, has translated "Verso" as "Near" every time. Now whether such uniformity is justified is a good question, but the question now is whether "Near Vienna" is apt for "Verso Vienna," and I think it is not, for the reason that "near" is too limiting a geographical marker. "Near" in the title of an English poem, as in

Hardy's "Near Lanivet, 1872" or Pound's "Near Perigord," has the effect of emphasizing the singular nature of the experience recorded in the poem by indicating that on the poet's private map the experience exists close to, but not at or in, the named place. "Near" is for an experience that took place somewhere that was cartographically nowhere. On the other hand, "Verso Vienna" obviously does not indicate that the location is Vienna. "At" is out. The trouble with "Near Vienna" is that while the encounter in the poem takes place in one place, just as importantly the encounter is presented as part of a journey. Instead of "Near Vienna," then, the translator might opt, as William Arrowsmith did, for "Towards Vienna." This seems to me no more correct than Galassi's choice, but for the opposite reason: "Towards" conveys the idea of a journey – as it does, for instance, in Ivor Gurney's "Towards Lillers," which includes the phrase "Lillers we approached" – but it does so at the expense of muting the poem's stress on its occasional nature.

What "Verso Vienna" calls for in English, then, is a word or a phrase that simultaneously expresses the two sides of the poem, location and movement. Curiously, in Richard Hugo's poem "G. I. Graves in Tuscany" we find these lines:

> I remember
> a washtub of salad in basic, blacktop acres
> of men waiting to march, passing three hours
> of bombers, en route to Vienna, and bombing
> and passing two hours of planes, coming back.[20]

To my mind, "en Route to Vienna" is just the phrase the translator wants. (However he got it, "*En Route* to Vienna" is the title Eamon Grennan gave his translation of "Verso Vienna," which is included in this book). Ben Belitt's title, "The Way to Vienna," might be preferable to "En Route" if it were changed to "On the Way to Vienna," and, given that Montale entitled his translation of "Sailing to Byzantium," "Verso Bisanzio," I am inclined to think that "While Driving to Vienna" might be the best title of all.

In 1980, in *Montale commenta Montale*, a question-and-answer book edited by its questioner, Lorenzo Greco, Montale disclosed that the setting of "Verso Vienna" is Linz.[21] This revelation allows us to read the opening lines of the poem more confidently, Linz being famous for its baroque architecture. But it also deepens our general perplexity. For in 1939, Linz in any European's mind was the town where Hitler grew up. "Find what occurred at Linz,"[22] Auden wrote that very year. What occurred there in March of 1938 was Hitler's return as conqueror. To the cheering crowds that lined the streets to meet him he declared: "If Providence once called me forth from this town to be the leader of the Reich . . ."[23] Since it had, Hitler planned to rebuild Linz as a cornerstone of the Reich.

Arshi Pipa arrived at his reading of "Verso Vienna" as a political allegory a dozen years before Montale revealed its setting to Greco:

The place names in titles such as "Verso Vienna" and "Verso Capua" conceal political events associated with these names. The event, for instance, to which "Vienna" refers is the Anschluss – the poem was written in 1938, the year in which Austria was annexed by Nazi Germany. "Afa" ("sultriness"), the word which concludes the poem, describes the political atmosphere of the time. The context in which the word occurs leaves little doubt: the poet sees in a "basset hound" barking at him the "only fraternal voice in the sultriness." The example illustrates the poet's moral isolation in a world in which the company of certain animals seems preferable to that of men. "Verso Vienna" conveys the poet's ominous fear of the alliance between Italy and Germany that had been concluded the previous year. The title may signify: "Toward a New Anschluss." The landscape in the poem is a baroque town somewhere in Central Europe, perhaps Switzerland.[24]

Although it seems to me that Pipa pushes his reading too far in regard to "Afa" and the title, and perhaps in regard to the dog (the poet's sense of solidarity with it is not, I think, a matter of its seeming "preferable" to the company of men), turning the poem into a more explicit commentary on political events than it is, his reading is essentially sound, and so turns the volume up on the poem's details.

Here is William Arrowsmith's translation, published in 1987:

> The baroque convent
> all biscuit and foam,
> shaded a glimpse of slow waters
> and tables already set, scattered here and there
> with leaves and ginger.
>
> A swimmer emerged, dripping
> under a cloud of gnats,
> inquired about our journey, spoke
> at length about his own, beyond the frontier.
>
> He pointed to the bridge before us,
> you cross over (he said) with a penny toll.
> With a wave of his hand, he sank down,
> became the river itself...
>   And in his place,
> to announce our coming, out of a shed
> bounced a dachshund, gaily barking –
>
> sole brotherly voice in the sticky heat.[25]

Until the ellipsis, this is really less translation than what Donald Carne-Ross has called transposition. Arrowsmith supplies an English facsimile of the sense of Montale's Italian, word by word, line by line. In his introduction to his translation of *Le occasioni* (*The Occasions*), Arrowsmith described his procedure this way: "When the Italian text gives *ridere*, I have translated it as 'laugh' rather than one of the more colorful modalities of laughter: chuckle, guffaw, titter, and so on."[26] Insofar as such strict fidelity to the Italian, the filling up of the page on the right by sliding onto it the words on the left, serves to give us an accurate rendering of the poem's sense, we must be grateful to Arrowsmith and applaud his work. That Arrowsmith altogether ignores the art of the Italian poem, or in any case makes no effort to reproduce it, is for the literal translator the necessary and honorable price to be paid for lexical accuracy. (Nabokov pronounced famously that it is the price the translator must always pay.[27]) The question is the degree to which this mode of translation can ever do what it promises.

Arrowsmith makes a number of apparently niggling and arbitrary changes to the poem. In line 2 he introduces an intensifier and an inversion not found in the Italian; in line 4, a tautology; in lines 6–9, a couple of reconfigurings of the relation of sentence to line. Worse, wherever the Italian is open to interpretation, Arrowsmith simplifies to explain the matter, for instance, making *corrente* "river" and treating *emerse* as a cognate: "emerged." The verb *emergere* does mean occasionally "to emerge," but it is used to depict an object breaking through water (a submarine, for instance, *emerse*), a usage no longer common in English (a submarine "surfaces"). In English, a person "emerges" from an enclosure, a man from a forest, say. The immediate sense, then, of Arrowsmith's phrase "A swimmer emerged" is to indicate not that the man appeared in the water out of nowhere, but that he got out of the water. But this is obviously at odds with Arrowsmith's translation of the later, corresponding word *sprofondo*, which he renders, "he sank down." If the swimmer gets out of the water at the start of the poem, then he would *dive* or *jump back* into it at the end. If he sinks down in the water at the end, then he never "emerged" from it at the start.

As is often the case with a literal translation, Arrowsmith's grammar is at times faulty, his diction dubious. What, for example, is the subject of "scattered"? Leaves may lie scattered, but can tables be "scattered with leaves"? (The OED calls this usage "rare," citing only Bloomfield's *Farmer's Boy, Winter 56*, 1798.) Why, too, is there a comma in line 9? And what is the grammatical relation between lines 10 and 11? As for the diction: What are "the slow waters" of a river? And does one "cross over" a bridge "*with* a penny toll" or *for* a penny or by paying a penny? The reader may now feel, as I do, that Arrowsmith's literalism hems him in so much that he cannot always be simply and movingly right in the one language that he and his readers share.

Arrowsmith's rendering of *d'oltre confine* in line 9 ought to give us the first real sign of what he thinks the poem is largely about. But although "frontier" will appear as one meaning of *confine* in any decent Italian/English dictionary, the word by 1987, the year of Arrowsmith's translation, especially for an American, signifies the part of a country beyond its settled part, or, secondarily, an unmarked border somewhere in unsettled or sparsely settled land. ("No one made a fuss here about frontiers, of how people crossed them: thousands of people – who could say how many – traversed frontiers which in their minds were no more than imaginary divisions" – Doris Lessing.[28]) Even more potent for a contemporary American is the sense of "frontier" as the outer limits of knowledge or achievement. Now, if the swimmer in "Verso Vienna" has made a "journey" into Nazi Germany, it would be inappropriate in the extreme to call that country "the frontier" in this last sense of the word. Arrowsmith does not say this. He says "beyond the frontier." Which seems to me wrong for two contradictory reasons: in 1939, the border between Germany and Austria (if that, in fact, is the border the poem has in mind) was an exactly demarcated one, though, on the other hand, following the Anschluss there ceased to be any effective separation of the two countries. It may be that Arrowsmith wanted "frontier" to suggest the moral wilderness that was Nazi Germany or Austria in 1939, but this would be only one of several of the suggestions made by the word here, and surely the faintest.

When Arrowsmith gets to the last three and a half lines of the poem, in which the Italian syntax is idiosyncratic, he is forced to strike out on his own. In just such a place does the literal translator have the opportunity to reveal his understanding of the poem and strut his own poetic stuff. Arrowsmith's lines seem to me wanting on both counts. He translates *posto* as "place" and *rimessa* as "shed," neutralizing the first (at a "frontier" we would expect to encounter a *battistrada* at his post, an available rendering of "posto") and making nonsense of the second. Why, in this setting, would the dog be in a "shed"? The crucial word, *battistrada*, means "outrider." Perhaps because he saw the difficulty of conveying the meaning of the Italian in just one English word, Arrowsmith introduces an explanatory phrase, "to announce our coming." Announce it to whom, and why? Evidently, Arrowsmith understands the dog to be an outrider in the secondary sense of a mounted attendant who rides in advance of or beside a car. But if we take *rimessa* to mean a carriage house, then the dog becomes a true "outrider": an officer of an abbey or convent, who attends to the duties of the community. The dachshund, then, is the embodiment of the place, a convent on the Danube in Catholic Austria, and the poet as he travels on will carry with him the memory of the dog's "fraternal" – a word, unlike Arrowsmith's "brotherly," fraught with the political and religious history of Europe – voice.

In *Collected Poems 1920–1954*, his translation of Montale's first three books, Jonathan Galassi singled out Arrowsmith as the friend and translator to whom he felt most indebted. Like Arrowsmith, Galassi adheres closely to the wording and salient content of Montale's poems. Many reviewers rightly applauded the selflessness and scholarship of Galassi's work. Here is his version of "Verso Vienna":

Near Vienna

The baroque convent
foam and biscuit
shaded a brief moment of slow water
and set tables, scattered here and there
with leaves and ginger.

A swimmer emerged, dripping
under a cloud of gnats, inquired
about our journey, going on
about his own across the border.

He pointed to the bridge in front of us
that costs (he said) a penny to cross over.
He waved, dove in again, became
the river...
        And, in his place
a happy dachshund, our pacesetter,
bounded barking out of a garage,

the one fraternal voice inside the heat.[29]

This does not differ much from Arrowsmith's translation, except
in its tone. More than Arrowsmith, Galassi, who is himself a poet,
seems intent on meeting the expectations of readers of poetry in
his country in his time. His phrasing is idiomatically up to date –
"a brief moment," "going on about his journey" – alert to the
character of the syntax of the Italian, and indifferent to the non-
prose side of the poem. (I hurry to point out that Galassi is not
always indifferent to formal matters.) Galassi's phrasing occasion-
ally comes up short: "Shaded a brief moment," for example, takes
the air out of Montale's inventive phrase, "adombrava uno
scorcio," not just because it fails to get more than a fraction of
what is expressed by the Italian, but because it is banal and tau-
tological. The hazards of ultra-idiomatic language are always
banality and tautology, and they are hazards that Montale's Ital-
ian avoids. On the other hand, Galassi's "going on about his jour-
ney" for *parlo a lungo* reminds us of one strength of the colloquial,
for "going on" nicely catches the strain of bored impatience one
hears in the Italian, not so much in the phrasing as in the abrupt
parataxis that marks the summary of the encounter in the middle
of the poem. By contrast, Arrowsmith's "spoke at length," though
it conveys the evident sense of *parlo a lungo* accurately enough,
fails to express the feeling in the phrase.

    Galassi's grammar is surer than Arrowsmith's, although the
comma after "And" in line fourteen is puzzling, and "scattered"
in line four is as detached from any subject as it is in Arrowsmith's

translation. What is most notable about Galassi's syntax is the degree to which, from the second line on, it exaggerates Montale's conciseness. His sentences miss the breathing intelligence of Montale's. In his brilliant essay, "Reading Montale," Galassi remarks that Italians hear in Montale's poetry "a nervous, astringent music."[30] Galassi, as I have said, seems to me to get this music into many of his translations (see, for example, the beautiful "Your hand was trying the keyboard" on p. 34 in this selection). In some cases, however, his English music is too astringent.

Galassi translates the keyword *battistrada* as "pacesetter." Evidently he agrees with Arrowsmith that the dog's duty is to ride alongside a car as an escort. I myself find it hard to imagine a dachshund doing this. Moreover, to a contemporary American, "pacesetter" invokes the world of racing – bicycle, car or foot.

Edith Farnsworth's translation appeared in her book, *Provisional Conclusions*:

Toward Vienna

The baroque convent
made of foam and biscuit,
shaded an inlet of smooth water
and well-provided tables, scattered
here and there with leaves and ginger.

A swimmer surfaced, dripping
under a cloud of gnats,
who inquired about our journey
and told of his voyages beyond the pale.

Indicating the bridge before us which
you cross (he said) with ten cents' toll,
he waved good-bye, and then submerged,
– he was the stream itself...

Understudy

in his place, a dachshund bounced
with a howl from a nearby shed,

sole fraternal voice in the sultry heat.[31]

Farnsworth knew Montale well and did her translations with some assistance and then approval from him. It may be that they discussed "Verso Vienna." This seems unlikely, though, because Farnsworth's translation is simply wrong at several spots and very odd at others. To begin with, the convent is not "made" of foam and biscuit. The image is visual and fanciful. ("So thick are the walls of Antioch ... Four hundred turrets surmount these walls, which are the color of biscuit" – Evan S. Connell.[32]) It stands to reason that the restaurant's tables were "well provided," but Montale says only that they were *imbandite*, "set." And the swimmer's gesture at the beginning of the third section, *Addito*, means only "He pointed." Nothing is gained, not accuracy, by dulling this to "Indicating." The whole line, "Indicating the bridge before us which," is ungainly.

At "surfaced" one's interest revives, for the word would appear to promise that Farnsworth is working with a comprehensive vision of the poem. Her swimmer does not emerge from, he suddenly comes up to the surface of, the water. It is his head, then, not his entire body, which is "dripping under a cloud of gnats." Translated this way, the figure becomes truly, eerily, Dantesque. Adding to the effect is "beyond the pale" for *del suo d'oltre confine*. Moth-eaten and out-of-poetic-bounds as it is for us, "beyond the pale" none the less gets at the idea of 1939 Germany as a benighted hinterland.

Why, then, does Farnsworth abandon this interpretation of the poem in the second half of her translation? *Sprofondo*, the image linked by the narrative and also by rhyme to the earlier image of the "dripping" swimmer, Farnsworth translates as "submerged," which keeps the swimmer in the water, but makes him behave too much like a submarine. Her next line, "– he was the stream itself ... ," states what the poem has already presented in an image, and has the effect of appearing to compensate for what was missed through overemphasizing the swimmer's oneness with *la corrente*, which Farnsworth inexplicably shrinks to a "stream." Worse still, *soldo di pedaggio*, which, as Pipa observed, recalls Charon's obolus, Farnsworth changes to a mere "ten cents' toll," fussily possessive. Ten cents may well have been the fare in American money in 1939, but it is mundanely meaningless in Montale's poem. "Howl" at the end suddenly resumes the Dantean theme, but then the dachshund turns cheerful and Disneyesque. Finally, "Understudy" for *battistrada*, like Galassi's "pacesetter," makes an unfortunate association.

Edith Farnsworth is a translator I admire much of the time. She has the ability to sustain the taut momentum of Montale's sentences, and she knows more words than most translators and betrays no reluctance to use them. For these reasons I have been delighted to include several of her translations in this anthology.

Ben Belitt's translation was published in 1964:

The Way to Vienna

The baroque convent
all biscuit and bubble,
shadowed a shred of slack water
where tables were set for the diners, here and there
scattered with ginger and foliage.

A swimmer appeared on the surface, waterdrops dripping
in an aura of midges,
ventured a question concerning our journey
and chatted at length of his own, into country beyond.

He pointed the bridge, just ahead; one crossed
(so he said) for a half-penny toll.
He waved with his hand, submerged,
was one with the current itself...

       And there where he floated

an outrider leapt from the coach-house –
a convivial terrier that yammered.

Single gregarious voice in the sultriness.[33]

We note four things right away. First, Belitt's sentences have a win-
ning confidence. Like the other three translators, Belitt keeps close
to the wording and shape of the Italian sentences, but he permits
himself more freedom to express, and so expresses more sensibly at
times, what the Italian essentially means. Second, though, we wince
at phrasing that makes little or only odd sense ("He pointed a bridge,"
"And there where he floated/an outrider leapt"). Third, Belitt sees
clearly and so is able to bring into focus some key images. This is
splendidly true of lines 6 and 7 and of the line, "an outrider leapt
from the coach-house –." Finally, despite his understanding of the
images, he injects into the encounter between poet and swimmer a
strange lightheartedness, as if the encounter were only a traveler's
tale. The menace in *d'oltre confine* dwindles to the "country beyond."

Belitt's second line, "all biscuit and bubble," introduces the
most remarkable aspect of the translation. Although it may be that
Belitt came to "bubble" through a knowledge of baroque architec-
ture, or by way of playing with *schiuma* (*bagna di schiuma* means
bubble bath), I suspect he discovered it prosodically, as part of his
metrical design. Belitt is the only one of the four translators of "Verso
Vienna" to attempt to re-create, or, rather, to find English equiva-
lents for, the verse of the Italian poem. Now and then his lines ap-
pear to be iambic, with frequent anapaestic loosening. But the verse
is accentual, not accentual syllabic. The stressed syllables are under-
scored by alliteration (and, just as often, consonance) as in Old En-
glish poetry:

A swimmer appeared on the surface, waterdrops dripping
in an aura of midges,
ventured a question concerning our journey,
and chatted at length of his own, into country beyond.

Translating "Verso Vienna" may seem an inappropriate time for echoing *Beowulf* and "Deor." But in an essay published in 1960, only four years, that is, before Belitt made his translation, Montale observed that in the poems in *Le occasioni* "the interweaving of rhyme and assonance is more compact" than in the poems in *Ossi di seppia*, and that he thought it strange that no critic had mentioned the influence on him of Hopkins. "In my own way," Montale said, "I was looking for my own 'sprung rhythm.'"[34]

In a review in 1948, John Berryman remarked that "experiencing a style is above all a question of hearing." Belitt's translation of "Verso Vienna" suffers from several shortcomings, some of which I have noted, but he deserves all praise for having heard the poem's style and for not being content to give a lineated trot. Berryman lamented in his review the presence then of what he called a "Climate" that was inducing in young poets, especially Americans, "*an acquired insensitivity to form*."[35] For forty years now this climate has existed as the pan-English ecosystem in which most translators, too, have worked. Its central conviction that, as one poet-translator put it in 1965, "formal devices have become a dead hand, which it is just as well not to lay on any poetry,"[36] still seems to many as right as rain. As readers of this anthology will now discover, I myself am far more sympathetic to what Edwin Morgan once termed "full translation," an ideal he glossed as "poetic sympathy linked with the care of accuracy."[37]

Notes

1. Jonathan Galassi, *Eugenio Montale: Collected Poems, 1920–1954* (New York: Farrar Straus & Giroux, 2000), p. 436.

2. Eugenio Montale, *The Butterfly of Dinard*, translated by G. Singh (Lexington: University of Kentucky Press, 1970), p. 5.

3. Eugenio Montale, *The Second Life of Art: Selected Essays*, edited and translated by Jonathan Galassi (New York: Ecco, 1982), p. 301.

4. Mario Praz, *The House of Life*, translated by Angus Davidson (London: Methuen, 1964), p. 211.

5. Henry Gifford, "An Invitation to Hope," *Grand Street* 3:1 (Autumn 1983), p. 298.

6. Praz, *The House of Life*, p. 210.

7. Mario Praz, "A Letter from Italy," *London Mercury*, vol. xxv, no. 147 (January 1932), p. 298.

8. Samuel Putnam, "A Miniature Anthology of Italian Poetry," *This Quarter*, vol. II, no. 4 (Autumn 1930), p. 568.

9. Bernard Wall, "From a European Notebook," *Changing World*, no. 7 (February/March/April 1949), p. 53.

10. Robert Lowell, *Imitations* (New York: Farrar Straus & Giroux, 1961), p. xii.

11. Elizabeth Bishop, *One Art: Letters*, selected and edited by Robert Giroux (New York: Farrar Straus & Giroux, 1994), p. 395.

12. Michael Hofmann, "Montale's Eastbourne," in *Behind the Lines: Pieces on Writing and Pictures* (London: Faber, 2001), p. 135.

13. Hofmann, *Behind the Lines*, p. 136.

14. Jeremy Reed, "Introduction," *The Coastguard's House: English Versions of the Poetry of Eugenio Montale* (Newcastle upon Tyne: Bloodaxe Books, 1990), p. 9.

15. F. R. Leavis, "Eugenio Montale's 'Xenia'," in *The Critic as Anti-Philosopher*, edited by G. Singh (Athens: University of Georgia Press, 1983), p. 151.

16. Jorge Luis Borges, "The Homeric Versions," in *Selected Non-Fictions*, edited by Eliot Weinberger (New York: Penguin, 2000), p. 69.

17. Arshi Pipa, *Montale and Dante* (Minneapolis: University of Minnesota Press, 1968), pp. 53–56.

18. *Eugenio Montale: Immagini di una vita a cura di Franco Contorbia*, edited by Franco Contorbia (Milan: Librex, 1985), p. 148.

19. Umberto Eco, *Interpretation and Overinterpretation*, edited by Stefan Collini (Cambridge: Cambridge University Press, 1992), p. 25.

20. Richard Hugo, *Making Certain It Goes On: The Collected Poems* (New York and London: W. W. Norton, 1984), p. 115.

21. Lorenzo Greco, *Montale commenta Montale* (Parma: Pratiche Editrice, 1980), p. 39.

22. W. H. Auden, "September 1, 1939," *Collected Poems*, edited by Edward Mendelson (London: Faber, 1994).

23. Alan Bullock, *Hitler: A Study in Tyranny* (New York: HarperCollins, 1991), p. 248.

24. Pipa, *Montale and Dante*, p. 53.

25. William Arrowsmith, *The Occasions* (New York: W. W. Norton, 1987), p. 19.

26. Ibid., "Translator's Preface," p. xii.

27. Vladimir Nabokov, "On Adaptation," in *Strong Opinions* (New York: Random House, 1973), p. 282.

28. Doris Lessing, *Ben, in the World* (New York: HarperCollins, 2000), p. 157.

29. Galassi, *Collected Poems*, p. 169.

30. "Reading Montale," in ibid., p. 417.

31. Edith Farnsworth, *Provisional Conclusions* (Chicago: Henry Regnery Co., 1970), p. 136.

32. Evan S. Connell, *Deus lo volt!: Chronicle of the Crusades* (Washington DC: Counterpoint, 2000), p. 32.

33. Ben Belitt, "Verso Vienna," *Quarterly Review of Literature*, vol. XI, no. 4 (Spring 1962), p. 254.

34. Montale, "Introduction to a Swedish Translation of his Poems," in *The Second Life of Art*, p. 318.

35. John Berryman, "Poetry Chronicle, 1948: Waiting for the End, Boys," in *The Freedom of the Poet* (New York: Farrar Straus & Giroux, 1976), p. 303.

36. Galway Kinnell, *The Poems of François Villon* (New York: New American Library, 1965), p. 20.

37. Edwin Morgan, *Beowulf: A Verse Translation into Modern English* (Berkeley, Los Angeles, and London: University of California Press, 1952), pp. v–vi.

TABLE OF DATES

1896 Born in Genoa, birthplace of Columbus, on October 12, Columbus's birthday. Montale is the fifth child of Domenico, an importer from Monterosso, and Giuseppina, the daughter of a notary in Nervi.

1905 Spends the summer at family's new villa in Monterosso, largest of the Cinque Terre, the five coastal villages, then all but inaccessible, between Genoa and La Spezia. He will spend the next twenty summers there.

1908 Attends school run by Barnabite Fathers. Baptized.

1910 First communion.

1915 Takes *bel canto* lessons with Ernesto Sivori, a Genoese baritone.

1916 Writes "Meriggiare pallido e assorto," the first of his poems, he remarked in 1946, "tout entier à sa proie attaché."

1917 August, after three medical deferments, undergoes a fourth physical examination, which he passes. Attends officers' training at Parma, where he meets Sergio Solmi, who will become his best early critic.

1918 Joins the Ligurian Brigade. Sent to a post near Valmorbia, a village in the mountains north of Verona.

1920 In Monterosso, meets the sixteen-year-old Anna degli Uberti, the first of his muses ("Arletta").

1921 Again takes voice lessons with Sivori. Suffers from unrelieved insomnia and nervous debility.

1922 Writes "I limoni" ("The Lemon Trees") and publishes other poems that will go into his first book. October, Mussolini marches on Rome.

1923 Sivori dies; Montale gives up the idea of a career as a singer. Anna degli Uberti spends her last summer at Monterosso. Autumn, Montale makes first trip to Rome. Mussolini's dictatorship emerges.

1924 Signs Benedetto Croce's anti-Fascist statement.

1925 Publication of *Ossi di seppia*, Montale's first book, by Piero Gobetti, editor, anti-D'Annunzian, and anti-Fascist, who the next year, at the age of twenty-five, will die in exile in France.

1926 Takes job as a copywriter with Bemporad, publishing house in Florence.

1927 Moves to Florence and joins group of writers and artists who gather at two cafés, Le Giubbe Rose and Antico Fattore. Writes to Mario Praz: "I have wasted years in various kinds of cures and spent thousands of lire. I have consumed hundreds of tonics, I have taken much ineffective Fellows syrup, I have had at least three thousand injections of glycerophosphates, sodium cacodylate, various formates, valerian and phosphates, etc., etc., without any result. So what? So there is nothing but to await a miracle and resign oneself to this hell. Sbarbaro told me that after 30 one grows out of these troubles: I am 31 and two months and I am worse."

1928 Publication of second edition of *Ossi di seppia*, with six new poems, including "Arsenio."

1929 Hired as curator of the Gabinetto Vieusseux, a research library in Florence. Lodges in the house of Drusilla Tanzi, a Triestine, and her husband, Matteo Marangoni, an art critic. Publishes translation of T.S. Eliot's "A Song for Simeon."

1931 Father dies. November, first interview with Montale appears in the *Gazetta del Popolo*.

1932 Publication of *La casa dei doganieri*, a chapbook of five poems; wins the Antico Fattore Prize for the title poem. August, visits London.

1933 April, Irma Brandeis ("Clizia"), a twenty-eight-year-old American Dante scholar, calls on him at the Vieusseux. August, travels to London, Eastbourne, and Paris.

1938 Marianna, his beloved sister, dies. May, Hitler in Florence. July, racial laws are enacted in Italy. December, forced to resign his post at the Vieusseux for failing to join the Fascist Party. Makes plans to join Brandeis in the States, to which she has returned, but does not leave Italy.

1939 Turns to translation, chiefly of Shakespeare's plays and American fiction, to earn a living. Moves with Drusilla Tanzi, known as Mosca for her littleness and nearsightedness, into an apartment on Viale Duca di Genova. Gives up for good the idea of going to the States. Publication of *Le occasioni*, his second book.

1940 June, Mussolini declares war.

1941 Montale ordered to submit to a physical examination at a military hospital in Florence; discharged as suffering from "sindrome neurosicastenica costituzionale."

1942 Mother dies in Monterosso. He writes "A mia madre." Family house in Genoa is destroyed.

1943 Publication, in Lugano, of *Finisterre*, a chapbook, smuggled into Switzerland by critic Gianfranco Contini. July 25, on order from King Vittore Emanuele, *carabinieri* arrest Mussolini. Winter, Montale takes in Umberto Saba, Carlo Levi, and other friends in need of shelter from the Germans.

1944 With Drusilla Tanzi hides out in friend's apartment during the battle for Florence. Tanzi hospitalized for acute spondylitis.

1945 After the war, joins the Partito d'Azione (Party of Action), which calls for national unity and proposes to be a third force in Italy between the Communists and Christian Democrats. April, founds with three other writers the journal *Il Mondo: Lettere Scienze Arti Musica*, which runs for eighteen months. June, Party of Action wins 1 percent of the vote in the national election. Spends first of many summers at Forte dei Marmi, resort in Versilia; while there, he begins to paint.

1946 At a conference in Milan, hears himself denounced as a metrical aesthete. Writes stories and sketches for *Il Corriere della Sera*, Italy's most important newspaper.

1948 January, during a visit to the offices of *Il Corriere della Sera*, writes in two hours the front-page article on Gandhi after word comes of the Indian's assassination. Appointed editor at *Il Corriere della Sera*. Moves to Milan, where he will live the rest of his life. Guest of British Council in England; meets T.S. Eliot at Faber & Faber. Publishes "L'anguilla" ("The Eel"). December, goes to Beirut to cover UNESCO conference.

1949 Meets poet Maria Luisa Spaziani, the "volpe" ("vixen") of the acrostical "Da un lago svizzero" ("From a Swiss Lake"), which he writes in September, and of subsequent poems. Publication of translation of *Hamlet*, made in 1943.

1950 Writes nearly a hundred articles this year, a total he will exceed each year of the decade.

1954 January, following report of Hemingway's death in a plane crash in Africa, writes obituary for *Il Corriere della Sera*. March, interviews Hemingway in Venice. Becomes music and opera critic for *Il Corriere d'Informazione*.

1956 Publication of limited edition of *La bufera e altro*, his third book of poems, and *Farfalla di Dinard*, a collection of stories.

1961 Receives honorary degree from the Faculty of Letters at University of Milan.

1962 Publication of private edition of *Satura*. July, Montale marries Drusilla Tanzi in a church in Fiesole.

1963 April, marries Drusilla Tanzi in civil ceremony in Florence. August, she breaks her femur in a fall; October, she dies in a clinic in Milan.

1964 January, invited to join Pope Paul VI's pilgrimage to the Holy Land.

1965 Takes part in celebrations of Dante's centenary in Florence and Paris.

1966 Publication, in an edition of fifty copies, of *Xenia*.

1967 Receives honorary degree from Cambridge University. Named Senator for life by President Giuseppe Saragat.

1969 Publication of *Fouri di casa*, a collection of his travel writings.

1971 Publication of *Satura 1962–1970* and a private edition of *Diario del '71*.

1973 Publication of *Diario del '71 e del '72*.

1975 October, wins Nobel Prize for Literature; December, delivers acceptance speech in Stockholm, "È ancora possibile la poesia?" ("Is Poetry Still Possible?").

1977 Publication of *Quaderno di quattro anni*. Made honorary citizen of Florence.

1978 Made honorary member of the American Academy of Arts and Letters.

1980 Publication of *L'opera in versi* (*Collected Poems*).

1981 Publication of *Altri versi e poesie disperse*. September 12, dies in Milan; state funeral in Milan; buried in Florence beside his wife.

FURTHER READING

By Montale

The Butterfly of Dinard, trans. G. Singh (Lexington: University of Kentucky Press, 1970)

Poet in Our Time, trans. Alastair Hamilton (New York: Urizen Books, 1976)

The Second Life of Art: Selected Essays, ed. and trans. Jonathan Galassi (New York: Ecco, 1982)

Selected Essays, trans. G. Singh (Manchester: Carcanet, 1978)

About Montale

G. B. Angioletti, "Italian Chronicle," *Criterion* (June 1927)

Anon., "Modern Italian Poetry," *The Times Literary Supplement* (21 June 1934)

Irma Brandeis, "An Italian Letter: Eugenio Montale," *Saturday Review of Literature* (18 July 1936)

—, "Eugenio Montale," *Columbia Dictionary of Modern European Literature*, ed. Horatio Smith (Columbia University Press, 1947)

Joseph Brodsky, "In the Shadow of Dante," in *Less Than One: Selected Essays* (Harmondsworth: Penguin, 1997)

Glauco Cambon, *Eugenio Montale's Poetry: A Dream in Reason's Presence* (Princeton, NJ: Princeton University Press, 1982)

—, "Summer Days with Eugenio Montale," *Canto* (Spring 1978)

D. S. Carne-Ross, "A Master," *New York Review of Books* (20 October 1966)

Joseph Cary, *Three Modern Italian Poets: Saba, Ungaretti, Montale* (Chicago: University of Chicago Press, 1993)

Henry Gifford, "An Invitation to Hope: Eugenio Montale," *Grand Street* (Autumn 1983)

Kevin Hart, "Eugenio Montale and 'The Other Truth'," *HEAT* 14 (2000)

Michael Hofmann, "Montale's Eastbourne," *Behind the Lines: Pieces on Writing and Pictures* (London: Faber and Faber, 2001)

F. J. Jones, *The Modern Italian Lyric* (Swansea: University of Wales Press, 1976)

F. R. Leavis, "Eugenio Montale's 'Xenia'," *Listener* (16 December 1973)

Jamie McKendrick, "Two Jackals on a Leash," *London Review of Books* (1 July 1999)

James Merrill, *A Different Person* (Westminster, MA: Knopf, 1993)

Eric Ormsby, "Jackals in Parentheses," *Parnassus*, vol. 24, no. 2 (2000)

Tim Parks, "A Prisoner's Dream: Eugenio Montale in Translation," *New York Review of Books* (4 February 1999)

Arshi Pipa, *Montale and Dante* (Minneapolis: University of Minnesota Press, 1968)

Mario Praz, "A Letter from Italy," *London Mercury* (January 1928)

—, "A Letter from Italy," *London Mercury* (January 1932)

—, "Italian Chronicle," *Criterion* (January 1938)

—, "T.S. Eliot and Eugenio Montale," in *T.S. Eliot: A Symposium*, eds. Richard March and Tambimuttu (London: PL Editions, 1948)

—, *The House of Life*, trans. Angus Davidson (London: Methuen, 1964)

G. Singh, *Eugenio Montale: A Critical Study of His Poetry, Prose, and Criticism* (New Haven, CT: Yale University Press, 1973)

Stephen Spender, "The Poetry of Montale," *New York Review of Books* (1 June 1972)

Bernard Wall, "From A European Notebook, 1948," *Changing World* (February/March/April 1949)

OSSI DI SEPPIA

Cuttlefish Bones

1925

JEREMY REED (b. 1951)

Reed, a prolific poet and novelist, was born in Jersey, the Channel Islands, and educated at the University of Essex. His first Montale translations appeared in *Selected Poems* (1987), in a section entitled "After Montale"; *The Coastguard's House* (1990) offers all his translations as "English Versions." Reed's most recent collections of poetry are *Saint Billie* (2002) and a book-length poem on Elvis Presley, *Heartbreak Hotel* (2003). In *Ossi di seppia*, the following poem stands first and in its own section called "In Limine," and is known by that title.

Be glad if the wind frisking the orchard
re-fires in you the need to live:
here, where a burnt-out circuit
of memories sinks,
was not a garden, but a burial-pit.

The throbbing you hear isn't flight,
but a tremor from the earth's core;
see how this solitary spit of land
flares into a crucible.

A blaze rages on the wall's nearer side.
If you go on, you will come,
perhaps, across the presence who saves.
It's here narratives are composed, and acts
deleted by the future.

If there's a loophole in the net,
accept that one blinding exit.
I ask this of you, go, for then my thirst
will lack the sharp corrosiveness of rust...

1990

JONATHAN GALASSI (b. 1949)

Galassi is a graduate of Harvard, where he was on the staff of the *Harvard Advocate*. Since 1976, when he reviewed Edith Farnsworth's *Provisional Conclusions* in the *New York Times*, he has been an un-flagging translator and interpreter of Montale. His translation of Montale's first three books, *Collected Poems, 1920–1954* (1998; rev. 2000), is a monumental work of scholarship as well as transla-tion. His other Montale translations are *The Second Life of Art: Selected Essays* (1982), *Otherwise: Last and First Poems* (1984), and *Posthumous Diary* (2001). He is the president and publisher of Farrar Straus & Giroux and Honorary Chairman of the Academy of Ameri-can Poets.

On the Threshold

Be happy if the wind inside the orchard
carries back the tidal surge of life:
here, where a dead web
of memories sinks under,
was no garden, but a reliquary.

The whir you're hearing isn't flight,
but the stirring of the eternal womb;
see this solitary strip of land
transform into a crucible.

There's fury over the sheer wall.
If you move forward you may meet
the phantom who will save you:
histories are shaped here, deeds
the endgame of the future will dismantle.

Look for a flaw in the net that binds us
tight, burst through, break free!
Go, I've prayed for this for you – now my thirst
will be easy, my rancor less bitter...

2000

BERNARD SPENCER (1909–63)

Spencer was born in Madras. He was at Marlborough College with John Betjeman and Louis MacNeice and at Oxford with Isaiah Berlin and Stephen Spender. From 1932 to 1940 he was a schoolmaster. In 1940 he joined the British Council and from then on usually lived abroad, in Salonika, Athens, Cairo, Madrid, Palermo, and Turin. His translations of four of Montale's poems, found among his papers and first published in *Collected Poems* (1981), were done in Italy.

The Lemon Trees

Listen, the poet laureates
move only among plants with unfamiliar names:
box or acanthus.
For me, I love the roads which find their way to grassy
ditches where in half dried pools the boys
catch a few famished eels;
the tracks which follow the slopes
descend between tufts of reeds
and end in the back gardens among the lemon trees.

Better if the clamour of the birds
vanishes swallowed in the sky:
clearer sounds the murmur
of the friendly branches in air that hardly moves
and the touch of this smell
which never quite leaves the earth
and fills the heart with a restless languor.
Here like a miracle the war
of the torn passions is silent
here to us poor falls our share too of riches,
the smell of the lemons.

See, in these silences when things
yield themselves and seem about to betray
their ultimate secret
sometimes the feeling comes
of discovering a flaw in Nature,
the dead point of the world, the link that does not hold
the thread to unravel which finally lands us
in the centre of a truth.
The eyes fumble round
the mind searches, tunes, parts asunder
in the scent which spreads like a stain
when the day gradually tires.
The silences in which one sees
in every human shadow that draws away
some disturbed divinity.

But the illusion fails and time brings us back
into loud cities where the blue shows
only in scraps high up between the eaves.
Rain tires the earth; the tedium
of winter thickens on the houses,
light becomes a miser – the soul bitter.
When one day through a half-closed doorway
among the trees in a courtyard
shines out the yellow of the lemons;
and the ice of the heart melts
and in our breasts peal
their songs
the golden trumpets of sunlight.

c. 1946–8

LEE GERLACH (b. 1920)

Gerlach is a prolific poet and translator, unreasonably overlooked by publishers. His one book is *Highwater* (2002). He grew up in Milwaukee and attended Wisconsin, Michigan, and (as a Stegner Fellow in poetry under Yvor Winters) Stanford. For nearly fifty years he has lived in southern California, a region whose topography rather closely resembles that of Liguria. Gerlach's translation of "I limoni," one of Montale's better known poems in Italy, appears here for the first time.

The Lemon Trees

Hear me a moment. Laureate poets
seem to wander among plants
no one knows: boxwood, acanthus,
where nothing is alive to touch.
I prefer small streets that falter
into grassy ditches where a boy,
searching in the sinking puddles,
might capture a struggling eel.
The little path that winds down
along the slope plunges through cane-tufts
and opens suddenly into the orchard
among the moss-green trunks
of the lemon trees.

Perhaps it is better
if the jubilee of small birds
dies down, swallowed in the sky,
yet more real to one who listens,
the murmur of tender leaves
in a breathless, unmoving air.
The senses are graced with an odor

filled with the earth.
It is like rain in a troubled breast,
sweet as an air that arrives
too suddenly and vanishes.
A miracle is hushed; all passions
are swept aside. Even the poor
know that richness,
the fragrance of the lemon trees.

You realize that in silences
things yield and almost betray
their ultimate secrets.
At times, one half expects
to discover an error in Nature,
the still point of reality,
the missing link that will not hold,
the thread we cannot untangle
in order to get at the truth.

You look around. Your mind seeks,
makes harmonies, falls apart
in the perfume, expands
when the day wearies away.
There are silences in which one watches
in every fading human shadow
something divine let go.

The illusion wanes, and in time we return
to our noisy cities where the blue
appears only in fragments
high up among the towering shapes.
Then rain leaching the earth.
Tedious, winter burdens the roofs,
and light is a miser, the soul bitter.
Yet, one day through an open gate,

among the green luxuriance of a yard,
the yellow lemons fire
and the heart melts,
and golden songs pour
into the breast
from the raised cornets of the sun.

2002

CHARLES WRIGHT (b. 1935)

Wright was born in Pickwick Dam, Tennessee. He has lived in Verona as a translator for the United States Army Intelligence Corps, in Rome as a Fulbright scholar, and in Venice as a Fulbright lecturer at the University of Padua. In addition to *The Storm and Other Poems* (1978), he has translated Montale's *Motets* (1981) and Dino Campana's *Orphic Songs* (1984). His poems, many of which draw on his experiences in Italy and knowledge of Italian literature, have been collected in *Country Music: Selected Early Poems* (1983), *The World of the Ten Thousand Things: Poems 1980–1990* (1990), and *Negative Blue: Selected Later Poems* (2000). The following poem appeared in *The Dream Animal* (1968). No American poet has been more influenced by Montale.

Portrait of Mary
(*After Montale*)

Mary, your twenty-odd years now threaten you,
A widening fog which, little by little, you enter;
Once in, we'll see you in its cloud-shapes and mist-shapes
Which wind, from time to time, will open or thicken.

Then from its swell, in passing, you will come
More white than ever, more multiple and new,
Clear, reawakened, and turning toward other things.
The winds of autumn rise; past springs still hold you.

Stretched out, face down, glistening with salt in the sun,
For you tomorrow's raw estate is welcome;
You call to mind the lizard motionless
On stone – youth traps you, her the child's grass snare.

The ocean is the force that tempers you;
We think of you as alga, a pebble, a creature
Which sea-wash and sea-salt can't lessen or corrode,
But return to the beach more perfect than before.

You shrug your shoulders; vast walls and castles crumble
Holding your future, loosing whatever will come.
You rise, walk out the small wood pier over
The creaking rise and fall, the suck of the sea;

You hesitate at the end of the trembling board,
Then laugh, and, as though knocked off by a wind,
You cut down to the water, which gathers you in.
We watch you, we who must remain ashore.

1968

DANIEL BOSCH (b. 1962)

Bosch is director of the Writing Studio at the Walnut Hill School. Handsel Books published his *Crucible* in 2002.

Falsetto

Esterina, your twenty years threaten you
like a grey-rose cloud
that little by little draws closed.
Yet its tightening doesn't frighten:
we see a girl who swims
under smoke the violent wind
rends, and gathers, and rends.
When the ashen swell expels you,
redder than ever, sun-fevered,
the arc of your back's a story, your face
Diana's kissed by her bow-string.
Your twenty falls climb
rungs of past springs;
the ringing in your ears
presages the Elysian spheres'.
Let no one break the clay pots'
cracked silence! What you should hear
is an ineffable concert
of tinkling bells.

Doubts about tomorrow don't scare you.
Graceful, taut on a wet rock,
glittering with salt, you burn
your limbs with sun.
Lizards are so fixed
on their bleak pedestals;
youth lies in wait for you

with a boy's noose looped from grass.
The power that tempers you is water,
in water you recover, in water, you are renewed:
we think of you as seaweed, as a pebble,
a sea-made sea-maid
brine purifies
and returns to the shore unscathed.

You couldn't be more right! The present
smiles – don't disturb it with worries.
Be gay – you have a date with the future
and a shrug of your shoulders
rocks strongholds, knocks over
dark towers tomorrows build.
You stand up and step to the slender
gangplank below which Gorgons screech:
your profile is etched
in silhouette against pearl.
You hesitate: the plank's highest edge trembles,
but then you laugh, a collapse
so complete it seems the wind has plucked you
or some divine friend taken you in his hand.

We are the race of watchers
who must remain on land.

2002

EDWIN MORGAN (b. 1920)

Morgan was born in Glasgow. He served in the Royal Medical Corps from 1940 to 1946, and from 1947 to 1980 taught English at Glasgow University. He was the first translator to produce a whole book of Montale's poems: *Poems of Eugenio Montale* (University of Reading School of Art, 1959). Donald Carne-Ross, noting seven years later that Morgan's book was "unobtainable," called the translations "impressively faithful to the poetic tone of the originals and to the literal sense." Morgan's Montales, both those of 1959 and those he made subsequently, are in *Collected Translations* (1996). His other books include a verse rendering of *Beowulf* (1952), *Wi the haill voice: 25 poems by Vladimir Mayakovsky* (1972; a translation into Scots), *Crossing the Border: Essays on Scottish Literature* (1990), and *New Selected Poems* (2000).

Sarcophagi I

Where will those curls be blown, and the young heads go
Of girls with shouldered pitchers overflowing,
Girls whose step is as light as it is sure?
Deep down a valley is opening
For their beauty in vain: shadow
Spills from trellises of vine
And the clusters droop in their swinging.
The sun pacing the sky,
The half-seen hill-slopes, lose
Their colours: in this soft-springing
Minute, nature is blinded
And steals through her happy creatures
As life, a mother indeed at whose dear will
Lightly all are dancing.
A world asleep or a world in old self-praise
Of its uninterrupted existence, who can say?

But give it, O passer-by,
The best twig that your orchard brings to birth.
Pass by: this valley is opening
Not to the mere succession of darkness and light.
It is far from here you must be led out by life.
Rest here, and refuge? No, you carry too much death.
Great gyres are yours, where you with your stars must go.
– And so goodbye, young curly-heads; goodbye so:
Going with your shouldered pitchers overflowing.

1959

Part two of *Ossi di seppia* consists of twenty-two short poems entitled "Ossi di seppia," which Italian critics often refer to as "ossi brevi," the short bones. Translations of eleven of the poems appear here.

JOSEPH CARY (b. 1927)

Cary is Professor Emeritus of English and Comparative Literature at the University of Connecticut. The following poem, which he has revised and lineated for publication here, was originally published as a trot in *Three Modern Italian Poets: Saba, Ungaretti, Montale* (1968). Cary is also the author of *A Ghost in Trieste* (1993).

Don't ask of us the word that squares on every side
our formless spirit, and in fiery letters
proclaims it and shines out like a crocus
lost in the middle of a dusty field.

Ah, that man who goes secure,
friend to others and to himself,
and has no care that his shadow
is stamped by the dog-star upon a crumbling wall!

Don't seek from us the formula that might open worlds
      for you –
rather some syllable as crooked and dry as a branch.
This only we are able to tell you today,
what we are *not*, what we do *not* want.

Meriggiare pallido e assorto
presso un rovente muro d'orto,
ascoltare tra i pruni e gli sterpi
schiocchi di merli, frusci di serpi.

Nelle crepe del suolo o su la veccia
spiar le file di rosse formiche
ch'ora si rompono ed ora s'intrecciano
a sommo di minuscole biche.

Osservare tra frondi il palpitare
lontano di scaglie di mare
mentre si levano tremuli scricchi
di cicale dai calvi picchi.

E andando nel sole che abbaglia
sentire con triste meraviglia
com'è tutta la vita e il suo travaglio
in questo seguitare una muraglia
che ha in cima cocci aguzzi di bottiglia.

[1916; revised 1922]

EDWIN MORGAN

This poem was first published in Morgan's *Rites of Passage: Translations* (1976).

Dozing at midday, dazed and pale,
beside a scorching orchard wall,
hearing the twigs and dry scrub make
a crack for the blackbird, a rustle for the snake:

spying on the ants in their red processions
over the tares or in wrinkles of ground,
now breaking file and now in collision
at the summit of some tiny mound:

watching far down through the leaves
the shimmering scales of the sea-waves
while shrill cicadas send their cries
quivering up from grassless crags:

and feeling with an unhappy wonder
in the dazzling sunlight where you've sauntered
that life and everything it labours under
is there in that wall you followed, with a shudder
looking up where its sharp broken bottles are flaunted!

1976

WILLIAM ARROWSMITH (1924–92)

Arrowsmith was educated at Princeton and Oxford, and went to Italy for the first time as a winner of the Prix de Rome. He published poems as a young man, but made his name as a translator and critic of literature and film. He was the first translator to bring Montale's first three books into English. His translation of *Satura*, edited by Rosanna Warren, appeared in 1998. He was the author of *Antonioni: the Poet of Images* (1995) and coeditor with Roger Shattuck of *The Craft and Context of Translation* (1961).

To laze at noon, pale and thoughtful,
by a blazing garden wall; to listen,
in brambles and brake, to blackbirds
scolding, the snake's rustle.

To gaze at the cracked earth, the leaves
of vetch, to spy the red ants filing past,
breaking, then twining, massing
at the tips of the tiny sheaves.

To peer through leaves at the sea,
scale on scale, pulsing in the distance,
while the cicada's quavering cry
shrills from naked peaks.

And then, walking out, dazed with light,
to sense with sad wonder
how all of life and its hard travail
is in this trudging along a wall spiked
with jagged shards of broken bottles.

1992

JONATHAN GALASSI

Sit the noon out, pale and lost in thought
beside a blistering garden wall,
hear, among the thorns and brambles,
snakes rustle, blackbirds catcall.

In the cracked earth or on the vetch,
spy the red ants' files
now breaking up, now weaving
on top of little piles.

Observe between branches the far-off
throb of sea scales,
while cicadas' wavering screaks
rise from the bald peaks.

And walking in the dazzling sun,
feel with sad amazement
that all life and its torment
consists in following along a wall
with broken bottle shards imbedded in the top.

1998

HARRY THOMAS (b. 1952)

Thomas is the editor of this book.

To pass the noon, intent and pale,
beside a scorching orchard wall,
and hear in the dry thorny brake
clicking thrushes, a rustling snake.

On the cracked ground or in the vetch
to spy on the red ants in files
that now break up and now crisscross
the pinnacles of little piles.

To see through leaves the distantly
palpitating scaly sea
as all at once from the bald peaks
rise the cicadas' tremulous screaks.

And walking in the dazzling sun
to feel with sad amazement then
how all we are and go through's in
this following a wall up on

the top of which jagged bits of bottles run.

2000

SAMUEL PUTNAM (1892–1950)

Raised in Rossville, Illinois, Putnam attended the University of Chicago for two years and then worked for fifteen years as a journalist in Chicago. In 1927 he moved to France. There he edited two of the legendary magazines of the twentieth century, *New Review* and *This Quarter*, wrote biographies of Rabelais and Marguerite de Navarre, and contributed articles on Italian culture to the *Saturday Review of Literature*. Between 1932 and 1935 he translated stories and plays by Pirandello, a novel by Silone, and the works of Pietro Aretino. He is still known to some as "the Cervantes man" for his superb translation, *The Ingenious Gentleman Don Quixote de la Mancha* (1949). The following poem was published, together with Samuel Beckett's "Delta" (see p. 62), in a special Italian issue of *This Quarter*. In his pro-Fascist introduction, Putnam describes Montale as "one of the best beloved of present-day Italian lyricists," and observes, "The dominant note in Montale is a cosmic despair."

Cuttle Bones
(*Poem for a Friend*)

Thought gives your smile again, a limpid stream,
glimpsed there by chance within its pebbled bed,
a tiny mirror for the ivy's clustered dream,
a calm, white, clasping heaven overhead.

Such my remembrance; for I cannot scan
your distant face: Is your soul frank and free;
or are you, world-flayed, one of those who flee,
and wear their suffering as a talisman?

So much I'll tell: your thought-given countenance
drowns fickle torments in a wave of calm,
and glides into my memory's graying glance
pure as the summit of a fair young palm.

1930

Portami il girasole ch'io lo trapianti
nel mio terreno bruciato dal salino,
e mostri tutto il giorno agli azzurri specchianti
del cielo l'ansietà del suo volto giallino.

Tendono alla chiarità le cose oscure,
si esauriscono i corpi in un fluire
di tinte: queste in musiche. Svanire
è dunque la ventura delle venture.

Portami tu la pianta che conduce
dove sorgono bionde trasparenze
e vapora la vita quale essenza;
portami il girasole impazzito di luce.

[1923]

BERNARD SPENCER

Bring me the sunflower so that I can transplant it
into my soil burnt with brine,
for it to show all day to the sky's mirroring blue
the anxiety of its amber face.

Things that are dark lean towards clarity
the bodies of things flow out and empty themselves
in colours: colours in music. Vanishing
is therefore the luckiest of chances.

Bring me the flower which leads
to the springs of transparent gold
where life like an essence turns to vapour
bring me the sunflower crazed with light.

c. 1946–8

EDWIN MORGAN

Bring me the sunflower to transplant here
in this briny ground of mine, in this parched place;
I want it to lift its anxious yellow face
all day to the azure eyes of the atmosphere.

Clarity is the care of things that are obscure.
Bodies exhaust themselves in running dyes:
the dyes in musics. To fade, I am sure,
is the adventure of all adventures that arise.

Bring me then the plant that points to those bright
lucidities swirling up from the earth,
and life itself exhaling what central breath!
Bring me the sunflower crazed with the love of light.

1976

JEREMY REED

The Sunflower

Bring me the sunflower and I'll transplant
it in my garden's burnt salinity.
All day its heliocentric gold face
will turn towards the blue of sky and sea.

Things out of darkness incline to the light,
colours flow into music and ascend,
and in that act consume themselves, to burn
is both a revelation and an end.

Bring me that flower whose one aspiration
is to salute the blond shimmering height
where all matter's transformed into essence,
its radial clockface feeding on the light.

1990

SONIA RAIZISS (1909–94) and
ALFREDO DE PALCHI (b. 1924)

Raiziss was the author of a critical study, *The Metaphysical Passion:
Seven Modern Poets and the Seventeenth Century Tradition* (1952),
and a book of poems, *Bucks County Blues* (1977). From 1960 until
her death she was the editor of *Chelsea*, long a home for transla-
tions of Italian poetry.

De Palchi was born near Verona, lived in Paris after the Sec-
ond World War, and then moved to New York. He is the author of
six books of poems in Italian, two of which, *The Scorpion's Dark
Dance* (1993) and *Anonymous Constellation* (1977), were translated
by Sonia Raiziss. With Michael Palma he edited *The Metaphysical
Streetcar Conductor: Sixty Poems of Luciana Erba* (1998). He is
senior associate editor of *Chelsea*.

Maybe some morning, walking in dry glass air,
I'll turn and see the miracle happen:
nothing at all behind me, at my shoulder
the void, and stare with a drunkard's terror.

Then as on a screen, the trees houses hills
will settle abruptly in the usual deception.
But it will be too late; and silent I'll go on
among men who don't look round, with what I know.

1962

EDITH FARNSWORTH (1903–77)

Farnsworth came from a prominent Chicago family. As a girl she studied violin with Mario Corti in Italy, but, convinced she had no future in music, returned to Chicago, taking degrees in literature at the University of Chicago and then in medicine at Northwestern University. She spent twenty-seven years on the staff of Passavant Memorial Hospital in Chicago, becoming a nationally known nephrologist. Mies van der Rohe built a weekend house for her in Plano, Illinois, the first house in the International Style in America. Following the house's completion in 1951, Farnsworth brought an acrimonious suit against van der Rohe for architectural malpractice, a suit she lost. Some years later she retired to Italy. *Provisional Conclusions* (1970) contains her translations of the poems from Montale's first three books not translated in Glauco Cambon's anthology, *Eugenio Montale: Selected Poems* (1965). She also published a translation of Quasimodo's poems, *To Give and To Have and Other Poems* (1969), and Albino Pierro's novella, *A Beautiful Story* (1976). She died in her villa at Antella, outside Florence.

> Valmorbia, blossoming clouds of plants
> were traversing your depths on summer breezes;
> flowering in us, by happenstance,
> oblivion of the world.
>
> The fusillades died down and in the lonely womb
> nothing resounded, other than the Leno's heavy boom.
> A rocket sprouted on its glowing stem,
> releasing burning tears, then dimming them.

The luminous nights were all a dawn
which ushered foxes into my grotto.
Valmorbia, a name – and now, in the bleak memory,
a land from which the night is gone.

1970

JONATHAN GALASSI

Your hand was trying the keyboard,
your eyes were following the impossible
signs on the sheet: and every chord
was breaking, like a voice in grief.

I noticed everything nearby turn tender,
seeing you helpless stalled unsure
of the language that was most your own:
beyond the half-shut windows the bright sea hummed it.

In the blue square butterflies
danced fleetingly: a branch shook in the sun.
Not one thing near us found its words
and your sweet ignorance was mine, was *ours*.

2000

DAVID FERRY (b. 1924)

Now the Sophie Chantal Hart Professor Emeritus of English, Ferry
was for many years the chairman of the English department at
Wellesley College. He is best known perhaps for his translation of
The Odes of Horace (1997) and his adaptation of *Gilgamesh* (1992).
Of his collected poems, *Of no country I know* (1999), Robert Mezey
wrote: "He has made poem after poem of surpassing honesty, clar-
ity, and beauty." The following poem first appeared in *Strangers*
(1983).

La Farandola dei Fanciulli

How far back the ancient past seems now.
Those kids dancing around and playing,
By the railroad track, up back of the beach,
On the gravel and cinders of the railbed,

Weeds suddenly breaking into blossom
In the heat of the day, a flowering of thirst.
It's as if being naked and nameless
Was being sunlight, flower, heat-shimmer.

1983

JAMIE McKENDRICK (b. 1955)

McKendrick was born in Liverpool. He worked for nine years at the University of Salerno. His books include *Sky Nails: Poems 1979–1997* (2000), *Ink Stone* (2003), and (editor) *The Faber Book of 20th Century Italian Poems* (2004). His poems in this volume appear in print for the first time.

At the crank of the windlass in the well
water rises to – and then becomes – the light;
and in the filled bucket's pristine circle
the image of a known face laughs and trembles.
No sooner have I leant towards those lips
that fade away than the past crumbles,
grows old, is someone else's...

                            Then the wheel
screaks, bestowing you, vision, back again
on the sheer black of the gulf between us.

EDWIN MORGAN

Peeweet

Peeweet, ye're a blithe-like birdie!
Whit makar has been fair to ye?
Yon whigmaleerie o a kaim gangs nid-nod
Heich on the hen-hoose-tap and whiles like the cock
Himsel ye swap aboot in the wind; "peeweet,
Peeweet": a sang and sign o spring – an O
But ye mak time dee to hear ye
And the girn and brattle o Feberarie,
And aa the airts gie a streetch
At the nod o yer heid, ma bird,
Ma spunkie, ma ferlie – and aa this is naethin to yersel!

1958

Peeweet: lapwing

Whit: what

Makar: poet

Whigmaleerie: fantastic thing

Kaim: comb

Heich: high

Whiles: sometimes

Girn and brattle: fret and turbulence, rain and wind

Ferlie: wonderful thing

SONIA RAIZISS

On the scrawled wall
that shades the random seats
the arc of the sky appears
complete.

Who any more recalls the fire that glowed
impetuous
in the world's veins – in chill repose
the opaque shapes are scattered.

Tomorrow I shall see the wharfs again –
and the wall – and the accustomed way.
In the future that opens, mornings
anchor like boats in the bay.

1958

Part four of *Ossi di seppia* is a suite of nine poems entitled "Mediterraneo" ("Mediterranean"). Six poems, translations of the second, fifth, sixth, seventh, eighth, and ninth sections, appear here.

ALLEN MANDELBAUM (b. 1926)

Now W. R. Kenan, Jr., Professor of Humanities at Wake Forest University, Mandelbaum was educated at Yeshiva University and Columbia. A recipient of the Order of Merit from the Republic of Italy, he has translated *Selected Writings of Salvatore Quasimodo* (1968), *Selected Poems of Guiseppe Ungaretti* (1976), and *The Divine Comedy* (1980, 1982, 1984). The three sections of "Mediterranean" in this book are revisions of the poems published in a special Montale issue of *Pequod* (Winter 1977), edited by Jonathan Galassi.

Ancient one, I am drunk with the call
of your mouths when they unfurl
like green bells that hurtle
back and peal.
The house of my far-off summers
stood beside you – you remember –
in the village where mosquitoes
cloud the air and the sun scorches.
Today, as then, I stiffen in your presence,
but I no longer feel
worthy of the solemn admonition
of your breath. You were the first to tell me
that the paltry ferment
of my heart was only a moment
of your own; that deep in me there lay
your hazardous law: to be
vast and diverse, yet fixed:
and so to empty me of all debris,
just as you thrust up on the shores,
among cork, seaweed, starfish,
the useless rubble of your abyss.

ALLEN MANDELBAUM

At times – suddenly –
the hour arrives when your inhuman heart
terrifies us, draws apart from ours.
Your music then does not accord with mine:
your every motion is my enemy.
And I fall back on myself, empty
of force: your voice seems dulled.
I stare at the stone debris that slopes
down to the crumbling, yellow coast,
streaked with sparse rainwater furrows,
that perches over you.
My life is this dry slope –
a means and not an end – a road
open to rivulets, to slow erosion.
And it is, too, this plant
born of devastation,
that faces the blows of the sea, suspended
among the wind's erratic forces.
This piece of soil that has no grass
has cracked that a daisy may be born.
In it, I sway toward the sea that lashes me;
silence is still missing from my life.
I watch the glittering earth;
the air is so serene as it grows dark.
And this that grows within me
is, perhaps, the rancor
that every son, o sea, feels for his father.

JAMIE McKENDRICK

Salt

We don't know if tomorrow has green pastures
in mind for us to lie down in beside
the ever-youthful patter of fresh water
or if it means to plant us in some arid
outback ugly valley of the shadow
where dayspring's lost for good, interred beneath
a lifetime of mistakes. We'll maybe wake up
in foreign cities where the sun's a ghost,
a figment of itself and angular
starched consonants braid the tongue at its root
so all sense of who we are is lost to words,
and nothing that we know can be unravelled.
Even then, some vestige of the sea,
its plosive tide, its fretwork crests will surge
inside our syllables, bronze like the chant of bees.
However far we've stumbled from the source
a trace of the sea's voice will lodge in us
as the sunlight somehow still abides in
faded tufts that cling to bricks and kerbstones
on half-cleared slums or bomb-sites left unbuilt.
Then out of nowhere after years of silence
the words we used, our unobstructed accents,
will well up from the dark of childhood,
and once more on our lips we'll taste Greek salt.

ALLEN MANDELBAUM

I should have liked to feel harsh and essential,
like the pebbles you spin,
gnawed by the brine;
a fragment outside time, witness
to a cold, unchanging will.
I was different: an intent man who watches
within himself, in others, the seething
of fleeting life – a man who delays
the act that, done, no one can then undo.
I wanted to search out the evil
that tarnishes the world, the trivial
flaw in the lever that blocks
the universal engine; I saw all
the events of a minute
as ready to disjoin in a downfall.
Having followed the track of one path, I had
the other's invitation in my heart; perhaps
I needed the knife
that severs, the mind
that can determine and decide.
I needed other books –
not your resounding page.
But I have no regrets: your song
again unravels the inner tangles.
And now your frenzy rises toward the stars.

JAMIE McKENDRICK

If I could just once syphon off
some tiny portion of your glorious rant
into this crabbed and arduous rhythm of mine;
if it was in my gift somehow to tune
my stuttering speech to your poliphony
– me, who once dreamed that I could plunder
those salt encrusted words of yours
where nature and art are not at odds
the better to cry out loud my melancholy
of a boy grown old who'd have done far better
not to think at all. But instead I'm left with
the stale stuff of dictionaries and this
clouded voice, prompted by love, and now grown weak
and good for nothing but plaintive literature.
All I have are these words like women
who donate themselves to anyone who asks,
these tired-out phrases that any moment
a crowd of student scribblers could snatch from me
and keep embalmed in their deathless verses.
Your thundering swells and looms and a fresh
shadow extends a fine blue stain. Put to the test
my thoughts desert me. Then my senses,
and with them sense itself – all sense of limit.

JEREMY REED

Then obliterate if you wish
the errors of a life,
as a sponge erases
the chalk marks on a blackboard.
I need to re-enter your circle,
find help in my fragmentation.
My coming here signifies
a meaning I lost on the road,
and these words of mine allude
unconsciously to a signal event.
But whenever the wind carried
your lazy surf upon a beach,
consternation shook me
as it does a man who's lost
then recollects his home.
Having learnt my lesson
more from the breathless gasping
of some deserted midday hour of yours
that is hardly audible
than from your glorious moment,
I give myself up in humility.
I'm no more than a spark from a beacon,
and well I know it, to burn,
this is my single, solitary meaning.

1990

NED CONDINI (b. 1940)

Condini was born in Turin. He was the recipient of the 1986 PEN/Poggioli Award for his versions of Mario Luzi.

North Wind

The skips of anxiety ruffling
the lake of the heart have disappeared:
gone is also that vast seething of matter
that blanches and dies.
Today an iron will sweeps the air,
uproots the bushes, manhandles the palmettos
and in the pressed sea sculpts
deep grooves crested with spray.
Every shape's bent in the roil of the elements –
one single howl, a lowing of torn lives.
The passing instant razes all.
What looks like leaves or birds fly through
the sky dome and are lost.
And you, all shaken by the whips
of the unleashing winds;
you who clutch to yourself
arms that are swelling with flowers yet unborn,
how hostile are the spirits
that overflow the convulsed earth in swarms,
my tender life, and how beloved are
your roots today.

1987

JONATHAN GALASSI

Eclogue

It was good getting lost
in the undulant gray of my olives –
talkative with bickering
birds and singing
brooks – in the old days.
The way the heel
sank in the cracked earth
among the silver
blades of tender leaves. Ideas
came to mind unorganized
in the all-too-quiet air.

Now the blue marbling is gone.
The local pine thrusts up
to breach the grayness;
a patch of sky burns overhead,
a spider's web
tears at my step: a failed
hour unlinks its chain around me.
Nearby, the rumble of a train
detunnels, swells. A shot
crazes the glassy air. A flight
pelts like a downpour;
instant, an armful of your bitter husk,
surges, goes down burned:
a pack of unleashed hounds
explodes in fury.

Soon the idyll will be born again.
The phase that hangs in the sky
gets recomposed, light streamers
slowly unfurl...;
                                the thicket of beans
vanishes, shrouded in them.
Swift wings are no help now,
nor bald proposals;
only the solemn cicadas
survive the saturnalia of the heat.
The image of a woman comes and goes
for an instant in a crowd.
She disappears; she wasn't a Bacchante.

Later, a crescent moon.
Backtracking
from our pointless wanderings
we could no longer read on the world's face
the trace of the frenzy
that lasted the afternoon.
Uneasily, we scrambled down
among the brambles.
In my country this is when
the hares begin to hiss.

2000

GEORGE KAY

Kay's *Selected Poems of Eugenio Montale*, first published by Edinburgh University Press in 1964 and then in an expanded edition by Penguin in 1969, was instrumental in making Montale's poetry more widely known in England. He also edited a valuable anthology, *The Penguin Book of Italian Verse* (1958).

Flux

The children with their little bows
terrify wrens in the holes.
The lazy blue trickles in the rill
that slothfulness grazes,
a rest stars grant the barely-living
walkers of the white roads.
Spires of elders tremble tall
and overtop the hill
commanded by a statue, Summer,
which stonings have made flat-nosed;
and on her there grows a redness
of creeper and a humming of drones.
But the wounded goddess does not look
and everything bends towards the fleet
of paper boats which slowly descend the trough.
An arrow glistens in the air,
fixes in a stake, quiveringly.
Life is this squandering
of banal events, is vain
rather than cruel.
                      They come back,
tribes of children with their slings
if a season's gone, or a minute,

and find dead features unaltered
even if all is crumbled down
and from its branch no longer hangs
the fruit they greeted.
– The children come back again ... like this, one day
the round motion that controls
our life will return the past to us
distant, fragmented and vivid, thrown
on unmoving screens
by an unknown lamp.
And still there stretches out
a hazy pale-blue vault
on the dense teeming of the watercourse:
and only the statue knows
time plunges and entangles
deeper by far, among the burning ivy.
And everything runs in the great descent
and the channel surges so wildly that
its mirrors crinkle:
the little schooners are caught and wrecked
in eddies of soap-foamed waste.
Goodbye! – stones whistle through the fronds,
grasping luck has made off again,
an hour slips, its faces dissolved,
and life is cruel rather than vain.

1964

ROBERT LOWELL (1917–77)

Lowell's ten annexations of Montale in *Imitations* (1961) first appeared in *Poesie di Montale*, a bilingual chapbook, with drawings by Giorgio Morandi, published in Bologna in 1960. This poem was found among Lowell's papers after his death and published for the first time in the *New York Review of Books*.

Flux

The children with their little bows
terrify the wrens into holes.
Sloth grazes the lazy, thin blue
sky-painted trickle of the stream –
rest from the stars for the barely
living walkers on the white roads.
Tall steeples of poplars tremble
and overtop the hardened hill
surveyed by a statue, Summer –
stonings have made her negro-nosed,
and on her there grows a redness
of creeper, a humming of drones.
The wounded goddess does not look,
and everything is bending to
follow the fleet of paper boats
descending slowly down the trough.
An arrow glistens in the air,
fixes in a stake, and quivers.
Life's this squandering of banal
occurrence; vain, rather than cruel.
They come back, if a season's gone,
a minute, these tribes of children
with bow or sling, and find the dead
features unaltered, even if

the fruit they grasped no longer hangs
dead on the young bough. The children
will return with the past for us,
distant, fragmented and vivid,
thrown up on an unmoving screen
by an unrevealed projector.
And still the hazy, pale blue vault
vacantly bridges the teeming
watercourse. Only the statue
knows what plunging, lost, entangled
things die in the burning ivy.
All is arched for the great descent:
the channel surges on wildly,
its mirrors crinkle; small schooners
are speeded, caught and wrecked in the
eddies of soap-foamed waste. Goodbye –
stones whistle through the thinning branch,
and gasping luck makes off again,
an hour slips, its faces dissolve...
life is cruel, rather than vain.

1981

MARIO PRAZ (1896–1982)

A Roman, Praz first went to England on a traveling scholarship in 1922. For ten years he taught Italian at the universities of Liverpool and then Manchester, before being appointed Professor of English Language and Literature at the University of Rome in 1934. While living in England he championed Montale's poetry, chiefly in "Letters from Italy" in the *London Mercury*. On visits to Florence during those years, as he later recalled in *The House of Life* (1958), an autobiography that centers on the furniture in his legendary apartment in Rome, "hardly a day passed" that he did not see Montale in cafés and restaurants. T.S. Eliot, who reviewed Praz's *Secentismo e Marinismo in Inghilterra* for *The Times Literary Supplement* in 1925, considered him "a great scholar." In his appreciative essay, "The Genie of the Via Guilia," Edmund Wilson remarked that Praz "should be considered as primarily an artist."

Arsenio
(*To G. B. Angioletti*)

Dust, dust is blown about the roofs, in eddies;
It eddies on the roofs and on the places
Deserted, where are seen the hooded horses
Sniffing the ground, motionless
In front of the glistening lattices of the hotels.
Along the promenade, facing the sea, you slide,
Upon this afternoon of sun and rain,
Whose even, close-knit, hours
Are shattered, so it seems, now and again
By a snappy refrain
Of castanets.

Sign of an alien orbit: follow it.
Then slide ye towards the horizon, overhung
By a leaden waterspout, high o'er the waves,
More restless than the waves: a briny whirlwind
Spumed of the unruly element 'gainst the clouds;
Tread on the rustling shingle,
And let your foot be trammelled by the weeds:
Maybe, your journey needs
This very moment, this long wished for moment,
To be saved from an end:
Your journey – link of an eternal chain –
A motion motionless, Arsenio, a too well-known
Delirious stir of immobility.

Listen, among the palm-trees, to the tremulous spray
Of violins, quenchéd when the thunder rolls
Clanging like many smitten iron plates:
Sweet is the tempest when in the blue sky
White rushes out the dog-star, and Eventide,
Which is so close at hand, seems still so far;
The thunderbolt, when splitting it, forth branches,
A precious tree within a rosy light.
The Tziganies' timbals are the silent rumble.

Along you slide, 'midst the precipitous darkness
Turning the noon into some strange midnight
Of kindled globes, whose oscillation spreads
Over the beach; and over distant places,
Where sky and sea melt into a solid shadow,
From scattered boats white throbs the acetylene –
Until the sky gives out in trembling drops,
The dank soil steams, everything, close by,
Is o'erflowed, the drenchéd tents are flapping,
An immense flurry skims the earth; down hurled
Rustle the paper lanterns on the streets.

So, lost among the wickers and the mats
Dripping, you, reed that drags along its roots
Clammy, never torn up, you shake with life,
You stretch yourself towards a resounding void
Of choked laments; the dome of the ancient wave
Swallows you up again, revolves you; again
All that takes you, street, porch, walls, mirrors, nails you

To a lonely, icy multitude of dead.
And should a gesture touch you, should a word
Fall at your side, such is perhaps, Arsenio,
In the dissolving hour, the lost appeal
Of some strangled life which rose for you; the wind
Carries it off with the ashes of the stars.

1928

EDWIN MORGAN

Arsenio

Tiny tornadoes lift the dust in the air
Till it eddies over the roofs and the empty spaces
Deserted by all except the vizored horses
That sniff the ground, transfixed, while in their faces
The windows glitter from the great hotels.
Down on the front, you go along by the waves
This day of rain,
This day of sun, with the refrain (sparkling
To confuse its moderation,
Its fine close net of hours) the castanets
Set clashing.

It's the sign of another zodiac you must steer for.
You must go down to a horizon overhung
By the lead-grey waterspout towering above depths
Less rootless than itself: a salty whirlwind
Spiralling up in the masterless chaos of weather
To the clouds: you must go where your footsteps
Squeak on the shingle and in the knotted tangle
Of the seaweed stumble: and that may be the instant
That time has so long lain in wait for, to save you
From the end of your journey, a link in the midst of
A chain, motionless progress, oh delirious
Memory, Arsenio, of marmoreality...

Listen! through the palm-trees comes a springing tremor
Of violins, quenched when the roll of thunder
With its beaten sheet-metal shatters the playing;
The storm is soft under Sirius, as the star
Of the dog-days is disgorged into the azure

Of heaven and far far off seems the evening
That is so near: if lightning comes to lance it
It branches out like a precious tree, through
Brilliant showers and dewy sprays: the distant
Gypsy drum is boom and silence too.

And down into the heart of darkness you go.
Steeply it descends, making midday a night
Of blazing globes put swinging to the sea,
And far out where a single shadow holds
Both sky and water, and a few boats blow,
Flaring acetylene unfolds –

                              until
The sky drips quivering, the soil steams as it drinks,
And you and the world around you are flooded and swirled
With the limp flapping of awnings and the gigantic sheets
Of whispering rain and the blown-down sodden shapes
Of paper lanterns scraping through the streets.

Here then are the drenched mats and rushes, and you
Yourself a reed among them, a reed that drags
Its roots where it goes, clinging and never freed,
You, trembling with life and yearning sent
Towards an emptiness ringing with broken lament,
The arch of that age-old wave that whirls you about
Becoming your gulf and vault; and here once more
Is everything that can recapture you – street and porch
And walls and mirrors – all that turns you to stone
Among the frozen lonely many dead,
And if one gesture can touch you, or if one
Word can become your friend, this is perhaps
A sign, in one spontaneous hour, Arsenio,
Of a struggling life ascending now through yours
And wind-borne with the ashes of the stars.

                              1959

WILLIAM WEAVER (b. 1923)

After graduating from Princeton, Weaver studied at the University of Rome. Since then he has been an indefatigable translator of Italian literature. He won the John Florio Translation Prize in 1968 for his translation of Pasolini's *A Violent Life* (1968) and the PEN Translation Prize in 1984 for his translation of Umberto Eco's *The Name of the Rose*. He is the author of *The Golden Century of Italian Opera: Rossini to Puccini* (1980). He lives in Italy.

House at the Sea

The journey ends here:
in the mean cares that divide
the spirit unable to cry out any more.
Now the minutes are even and fixed
like the wheel-turns of the pump.
One turn: a gush of resounding water.
Another: more water, at times a creaking.

The journey ends on this beach
tried by the slow and constant waves.
The seashore reveals nothing save lazy wisps
of smoke and the soft gusts
weave it with hollows; and rarely
in the mute calm
through the wandering islands of the air
Capraia appears or spiny Corsica.

You ask if everything vanishes thus
in this scant mist of memories;
if in the benumbed hour or in the sigh
of the surf every destiny is fulfilled.

I would like to say no, that the hour is near
when you will pass beyond time;
perhaps only he who wills it makes himself infinite,
and who knows? – you may do this. Not I.
I think that for the most there is no salvation,
but let someone disrupt all patterns,
scale the pass, find himself as he wants.
I would like before giving in to point out to you
this avenue of escape,
unsteady, as foam or wrinkle
in the shaken fields of the sea,
I give you also my miserly hope.
In these new days, weary, I cannot enlarge it:
I offer it in pledge to your fate, that it save you.

The road ends on these banks
that the tide with alternate motion gnaws.
Your heart, near me, not hearing,
is perhaps already setting sail for the eternal.

1974

CHARLES WRIGHT

The Dead

The sea that breaks on the opposite shore
throws up a cloud that spumes
until the sand flats reabsorb it. There,
one day, we jettisoned, on the iron coast,
our hope, more gasping than
the open sea – and the sterile abyss turns green
as in the days that saw us among the living.

Now that the north wind has flattened out the cloudy tangle
of gravy-colored currents and headed them back
to where they started, all around someone has hung,
on the limbs of the tree thicket, fish nets that string
along the path that goes down
out of sight;
faded nets that dry in the late
and cold touch of the light; and over them
the thick blue crystal of the sky winks
and slides toward a wave-lashed arc
of horizon.
            More than seawrack dragged
from the seething that uncovers us, our life
moves against such stasis: and still it seethes
in us, that one thing which one day stopped, resigned
to its limits; among the strands that bind
one branch to another, the heart struggles
like a young marsh hen
caught in the net's meshes;
and motionless and migratory it holds us,
an icy steadfastness.
                  Thus

maybe the dead too have all rest taken away from them
in the ground; a force more pitiless
than life itself pulls them away from there, and all around
(shadows gnawed and swallowed by human memories)
drives them to these shores, breaths
without body or voice
betrayed by the darkness;
and their thwarted flights brush by us even now,
so recently separated from us, so close still,
and back in the sea's sieve go down...

2000

SAMUEL BECKETT (1906–89)

When he graduated from Trinity College, Dublin, in 1927, Beckett stood first in his class in modern languages. In Paris in 1930, he signed on as editor and translator of the Italian section of Samuel Putnam's anthology of new prose and poetry, *The European Caravan* (1931). For want of money, the section was left unpublished, but the translation that follows appeared in Putnam's magazine, *This Quarter*, along with Beckett's translations of poems by Rafaello Franchi and Giovanni Comisso. His books include *Collected Poems 1930–1978* (1984) and *An Anthology of Mexican Poetry* (1958), translated by Beckett and compiled and introduced by Octavio Paz. He was awarded the Nobel Prize in 1969.

Delta

To thee
I have willed the life drained
in secret transfusions, the life chained
in a coil of restlessness, unaware, self-angry.

When time leans on his dykes
then thine
be his allconsciousness
and memory flower forth in a flame
from the dark sanctuary, and shine
more brightly, as now, the rain over, the dragon's-blood
on the walls and the green against the branches.

Of thee
I know nothing, only
the tidings sustaining my going,

and shall I find
thee shape or the fumes of a dream
drawing life
from the river's fever boiling darkly
against the tide.

Of thee nothing in the grey hours and the hours
torn by a flame of sulphur,
only
the whistle of the tug
whose prow has ridden forth into the bright gulf.

1930

DESMOND O'GRADY (b. 1935)

O'Grady was born in Limerick, Ireland. When he was twenty-one, living in a silent Cistercian monastery off the coast of Wales, he received out of the blue two letters and $50 from Ezra Pound. The next summer O'Grady moved to Rome. He was at the dock in Naples to greet Pound at the end of his voyage from St Elizabeth's. For periods he taught in Rome, and twice studied Celtic literature at Harvard (MA 1964; Ph.D. 1982). The author of many books of poems, he is best known for his translations from several languages, now collected in *Trawling the Traditions* (1994). He had a small part in Fellini's *La dolce vita*.

Delta

I have harnessed that life
which explodes in secret effusions
to you, that life which,
at odds within itself, seems
not to know you – muffled as you are
in your own presence.

Memory, when time rises against its dykes
you attune your vicissitude to its immensity
and surface more revealed
from the dark you descended into –
just as now, after rain, the green of the branches,
the wash on the walls, deepens again.

Whether you exist as a particular form
or whether you are a delusion, nourished
in the vapours of a dream by the fevered,

troubled seaboard thundering against the tide,
I know nothing of you beyond the mute
message that sustains me on my way.

Know nothing of you in the vacillation
of the grey hours, or of those ripped by a sulphur flame,
nothing but the hooting through mist
of a tug finding its dock in the gulf.

1965

LE OCCASIONI

The Occasions

1939

BEN BELITT (b. 1911)

Belitt taught for several decades at Bennington College. His recent books are *The Forged Feature: Toward a Poetics of Uncertainty: New and Selected Essays* (1994) and *This Scribe, My Hand: The Complete Poems* (1998). *Adam's Dream: A Preface to Translation* (1978) contains his good essay on Lowell's translations of Montale, "Lowell's *Imitations*: Translation as Personal Mode." He is well known for his translations of the poems of Neruda and Alberti.

The Balcony

The gambit seemed easy –
a change to annihilate space
where it opened for me: the blaze
of your certainty turned into quizzical tedium.

Now I contract, in that void,
all my tardy volition:
out of bitter non-being there flashes
the will to attend you, alive.

That life, shedding lustre –
you acknowledged no other –
you lean to it now from that window
which never grows lighter.

1962

Lindau

La rondine vi porta
fili d'erba, non vuole che la vita passi.
Ma tra gli argini, a notte, l'acqua morta
logora i sassi.
Sotto le torce fumicose sbanda
sempre qualche ombra sulle prode vuote.
Nel cerchio della piazza una sarabanda
s'agita al mugghio dei battelli a ruote.

[1932]

EDWIN MORGAN

Lindau

Brought by the swallow,
These blades of grass; he wants no grim blowclocks.
But at night by the dykes, the sluggish waters hollow
And obliterate rocks.
Every moment the smoking torches father
Some shadow that glides off over the lifeless banks.
Within the square saraband-dancers gather,
Swaying to the paddle-steamers' chugs and clanks.

1959

BEN BELITT

Lindau

The swallow, that life may not fail,
comes there with his grass-blade.
But over the jetties at night a dead water
wears through the shale.
Always in torch-smoke
the darkness divides on the void of the shore-line.
In the round of the plaza a sarabande
stirs: the wheels of the paddle-boats wail.

1962

JEREMY REED

Lindau

Unfailingly the swallow maintains life,
returning here beak needling with a straw.
At night by the piers, slack water
sluggishly wears through the eroding shale.
Torches smoke, their gusty shadows
played out fluently on the lifeless shore.
In the plaza a saraband strikes up.
Listen, the wheels of the paddleboats wail.

1990

G. S. FRASER (1915–80)

Fraser was born in Glasgow, and won a scholarship at St Andrews University on the basis of his gift for languages. He spent the war in Egypt, where he came to know Bernard Spencer, Keith Douglas, Lawrence Durrell, and other writers connected with *Personal Landscape*, and in Ethiopia, where he edited a half-English, half-Italian newspaper, the *Eritrean Daily News* (*Il Quotidiano Eritreo*). In London after the war he was a prominent reviewer, literary historian, translator, and anthologist. He translated parts of Dante's *Inferno* and *Paradiso* for the BBC's Third Programme in 1966. He taught at the University of Leicester from 1964 until his death.

Bagni di Lucca

Between the thud of the falling chestnuts
And the groan of the torrent
That unite their sounds
The heart hesitates.

Premature winter that the north wind
Shudders through! I present myself
At the ledge which lets loose the twilight
Of the day into the ice.

Marbles, branchings –
               and at a shaking
Leaves in spirals, like arrows,
Into the ditch.

There passes the last herd, lost in the mist
Of the beasts' own breath.

1965

EAMON GRENNAN (b. 1941)

Grennan has a degree in English and Italian from University College, Dublin, and teaches at Vassar. He has lived in Italy. In 1997 he published *Leopardi: Selected Poems* (1997). His most recent book is *Relations: New and Selected Poems* (1998). His translations in this book are published for the first time.

En Route to Vienna

The baroque convent, all meerschaum and biscuit,
shaded a glimpse
of slow-moving water and laid tables,
strewn here and there with leaves
and lumps of ginger.

A swimmer emerged, shook himself
under a gnat-cloud,
inquired of our journey,
spoke at length of his own, over the border.

He pointed to the near bridge
which can be crossed (so he told us)
for a penny. He waved, dived,
was the stream itself...
                        And in his stead –
blazing the way for us – a little dachshund
bounded out of a garage, barking with joy,

one brotherly voice in the sultry haze.

EDITH FARNSWORTH

Toward Capua

...its spine broken at the curve, with a leap
the blonde Volturno fell, pouring its
floods over the heath and dispersing them
into crevices. Farther down, the profile
of a coachman moved above the hedgerows,
appearing as if on horses,
in a train of dust and jingling bells.
It stopped a moment; the equipage lurched;
everywhere there fluttered the tiniest
of butterflies. Then a furtive beam
lighted the battered grove of cork trees:
laboriously the coach departed; and you
inside, again and ever again waving
a scarf, the starry banner in your hand!
– and the gluttonous river was lost in sand.

1970

MAURICE ENGLISH (1909–83)

English was born in Chicago. After graduating from Harvard in 1933, he spent several years as a foreign correspondent in Europe. From 1953 he worked at the University of Chicago Press, Temple University Press, which he founded, and finally the University of Pennsylvania Press. He was the author of two books of poems, *Midnight in the Century* (1964) and *A Savaging of Roots* (1974). Montale admired his translations, including, presumably, this one, which was first published in Selden Rodman's splendid anthology, *100 Modern Poets* (1949).

Dora Markus

I

We stood where the wooden piers
at Porto Corsini lead to the open sea,
and a few fishermen, with scarcely a motion,
cast and drew in their nets. Raising your hand
you pointed to the opposite shore
invisible, your true homeland.
Then we followed the canal to the flatlands
where the city docks
lie shining and sooty, and a sluggish
springtime sank without memory.

And here where an ancient humanity
dissolves itself into a soft
and Orient anxiety,
your words glistened like the coppery scales
of a fish, glistening and dying.

That restlessness of yours recalls to me
those migratory birds which hurl themselves at the pharos

on stormy evenings:
your gentleness too is a kind of tempest,
invisible, wrapped in stormwinds,
in its moments of tranquillity most rare.
I do not know how, exhausted, you survive
in that lake of indifference
which is your heart: perhaps
what saves you is a talisman you keep
jumbled with the lipstick,
powderpuff and nailfile in your bag: a white mouse,
carved in ivory: and so you exist!

2

And now in your Carinthia
of flowered myrtles and still lagoons,
stooped at the water's edge, you watch
the carp's shy nibbling at the bait
or trace on linden trees, between
their shaggy pinnacles, the flare
of evening, its glow reflected on the waters
from the quayside awnings and the shore hotels.

The evening which flows out
across the damp flatlands, brings with it
only the palpitation of motors and
the honking of geese, and a room
gleaming with snow-white majolica tells
to the tarnished mirror, which saw you
otherwise, a story of imperturbable
errors, and engraves it there
where nothing can erase it.

Your legend, Dora!
But it is written already in the glances

of those men whose haughty mustaches droop
in their great portraits framed in gold, its refrain
comes back at every chord struck
from the toneless keyboard in the hour
which darkens and grows always later.

It is written there. At the kitchen sill
the evergreen laurel
endures, the voice does not change,
Ravenna is far away, a ferocious faith
distills its venom.
What does it ask of you? The voice,
the legend, the destiny: these have no end...
But the hour is late, and grows always later.

1949

ALFRED CORN (b. 1943)

Corn has published several books of poems, from *All Roads at Once* (1976) to *Present* (1997). His essay, "The Anglo-Italian Relationship: Eugenio Montale," appears in *The Metamorphoses of Metaphor: Essays in Poetry and Fiction* (1987).

Dora Markus

I

It was where the wooden bridge
crosses to Porto Corsini on the open sea
and a few men, in slow motion, lower
or haul in their nets. With a wave
of your hand you gestured toward the other
invisible shore, your true homeland.
Then we followed the canal as far as the wharves
of the town, glistening with soot,
in that lowland where a cold spring
slowly settled down, outside memory.

And here, where a classical age
begins to break up under delicate
Asiatic tensions,
your words shimmered like rainbows on the scales
of a trout drowning in air.

Your restlessness calls to mind
birds of passage that crash against lighthouses
on stormy nights –
but your tenderness, too, is a storm,
always lowering, never breaking;
and its lulls are rarer still.

Pushed so far, how do you stay
afloat in that lake
of indifference, your heart? Perhaps
an amulet protects you, one you keep
next to your lipstick, your nail-file,
your compact: a white mouse,
in ivory. *Somehow you survive!*

2

Now, in your Carinthia,
with its flowering myrtles and little ponds,
leaning over the edge you look down
at the timid carp that gapes and swallows;
or stroll under the lindens, their crowns
thrusting up into sunset
bonfires, the waters ablaze
with awnings of landings and hotels.

The evening that stretches out
over a misty inlet brings,
above the stutter of motors,
only the cries of geese; and an interior
of snowy tiles tells
the blackened mirror that hardly
recognized you a story of errors
calmly acknowledged, engraving it within
where the dustcloth doesn't reach.

Your golden legend, Dora –
but it is already written in the fixed stares
of those men with fluffy sidewhiskers,
dignified and weak, portraits
in big, gilt frames; a refrain
that comes back with every chord wrung

from the cracked barrel-organ at the hour
when dusk falls, always later and later.

It is written there. The evergreen
bayleaf all through the kitchen
survives, the voice does not fail,
Ravenna is far away; and a barbarous
creed keeps secreting its poison.
What can it want from you? None surrenders,
voice, legend, nor destiny...
But it is late, always later and later.

1983

Part two of *Le occasioni* is a series of twenty "Mottetti" ("Motets"), which Montale once called an "autobiographical novelette." Translations of the first (2), second, third, sixth (2), seventh (2), fifteenth, sixteenth (2), nineteenth, and twentieth (2) of the poems appear here. The Italian original of the first is also included.

Lo sai: debbo riperderti e non posso.
Come un tiro aggiustato mi sommuove
ogni opera, ogni grido e anche lo spiro
salino che straripa
dai moli e fa l'oscura primavera
di Sottoripa.

Paese di ferrame e alberature
a selva nella polvere del vespro.
Un ronzìo lungo viene dall'aperto,
strazia com'unghia ai vetri. Cerco il segno
smarrito, il pegno solo ch'ebbi in grazia
da te.
            E l'inferno è certo.

JONATHAN GALASSI

You know: I have to give you up again
and I can't. Each action, every shout
jars me like a perfect shot,
even the salt breeze that floods the wharves,
and breeds the lightless spring
of Sottoripa.

Land of ironwork and mast-
forests in the evening dust.
A long drone enters from outside,
torments like a fingernail on glass.
I'm after the lost sign, the single
pledge you graced me with.
                              And hell is certain.

                                          2000

ARSHI PIPA (1920–95?)

Pipa was born in Scutari, Albania, and educated at the University of Florence. For many years he was the Director of Graduate Studies in Italian at the University of Minnesota. He wrote several books of poems and scholarship in Albanian. The following poem appears in his *Montale and Dante* (1968).

Many years, and a harder one by the foreign
lake on which the sunsets burn.
Then you descended from the mountains to bring back to me
Saint George and the Dragon.

Would that I might stamp them on the flag
that waves in the lashing northeast wind
in the heart ... And descend for you in a gulf
of fidelity, immortal.

1968

J. D. McCLATCHY (b. 1945)

McClatchy has published four books of poetry, including *Stars Principal* (1984), in which the two poems printed in this book were published, a book of essays, and several libretti. He is the editor of the *Yale Review*.

Rime at the panes; the patients
always enclosed, always at loose
ends; and over the tables
endless readings of the cards.

Your exile, say. Again I think
over mine, and of the morning
when I heard between the cliffs
that ballerina bomb shuffling.

The nightly game, the fireworks,
took forever: as if a holiday.

Then a rough wing grazed my hand,
but to no end: this is not your card.

1984

JEREMY REED

I'd lost the hope of seeing you again,
you'd travelled far, a fish gone with the line,
leaving me to face a blizzarding screen
of images, like those that precede death.
If something of you remained, protean,
tenuous, lit by a moment's dazzle,
it was in this sharp cameo –

(At Modena, between the porticoes,
a liveried servant tightened his grip,
dragging two jackals on a leash).

1990

DANA GIOIA (b. 1950)

Gioia is a Californian. He has degrees from Stanford and Harvard. He has written two books of poems, *Daily Horoscope* (1986) and *The Gods of Winter* (1991), and a volume of essays, *Can Poetry Matter?* (1992), and has coedited *Poems from Italy* (1985) and *New Italian Poets* (1991). His translation of the "Mottetti," *Mottetti: Poems of Love*, came out in 1990.

I had almost lost
hope of ever seeing you again;

and I asked myself if this thing
cutting me off
from every trace of you, this screen
of images,
was the approach of death, or truly
some dazzling
vision of you
out of the past,
bleached, distorted,
fading:

(under the arches at Modena
I saw an old man in a uniform
dragging two jackals on a leash).

1990

JEREMY REED

In undulating flights martins reveal
their black and white plumage, frenetically
tripping from telegraph wires to the sea.
You lift your eyes for some consolation,
disconsolately standing on the quay.

Already the elder tree's foam
of umbels anchor their perfume above
earth turned from an excavation.
The squall stands off, but calm's an illusion,
your threat hums like the fin-tip of a shark...

1990

DANA GIOIA

At dawn, when suddenly
the noise of a train
speeding through a tunnel
tells me of the men on journeys
trapped in stone,
lit only now and then
by a flash of sky and water:

at dusk when the woodworm
eating slowly through the desk
redoubles its efforts,
and the footsteps of the watchman
come closer:
at dawn and at dusk, even these
moments become human, if you
weave them together with your thread.

1990

J. D. McCLATCHY

The flower that rehearses
at the edge of the gorge
its forget-me-not
has no strain more joyous, more clear
than what emptiness we bridge.

A rasp of iron comes between us,
the pig-headed azure won't return.
In a palpable heat the funicular drops me
at the opposite station, already dark.

1984

DANA GIOIA

The flower on the mountainside,
which keeps repeating its
forget-me-nots from cliff
to cliff, has no colors brighter
or happier than the space
set between us.

A screech of metal is pulling us apart.
The obstinate blue is fading. In a sky
so sultry you can barely
see through it, the funicular
carries me back to the other station
where it's already dark.

1990

KATE HUGHES

Hughes's *Xenia and Motets* was published in 1972.

Do not, o scissors, cut off that face,
alone in my diminished memory,
don't turn that wide look as she listened, intent,
into my unending mist.

A chill descends ... Bitter the severing blow.
And the wounded acacia shakes off
the cicadas husk
into the early mire of November.

1980

KATE HUGHES

...but so be it. The cornet
talks it over with the bee-swarms in the oak.
On the seashell where the evening glows
a painted volcano gaily puffs up smoke.

So too the coin set in lava
shines on the table where it holds down
these meagre sheets. And life that seemed vast
is briefer than your handkerchief.

1980

JEREMY REED

...so be it. The sound of a cornet
answers the hiving bee-swarms in the oak.
On the carved seashell where a gold light falls,
a painted volcano eructates smoke.

On the table the lava paperweight
with its embedded coin holds down a sheaf
of manuscript. The life I thought so vast
is briefer than your handkerchief.

1990

La casa dei doganieri

Tu non ricordi la casa dei doganieri
sul rialzo a strapiombo sulla scogliera:
desolata t'attende dalla sera
in cui v'entrò lo sciame dei tuoi pensieri
e vi sostò irrequieto.

Libeccio sferza da anni le vecchie mura
e il suono del tuo riso non è più lieto:
la bussola va impazzita all'avventura
e il calcolo dei dadi più non torna.
Tu non ricordi; altro tempo frastorna
la tua memoria; un filo s'addipana.

Ne tengo ancora un capo; ma s'allontana
la casa e in cima al tetto la banderuola
affumicata gira senza pietà.
Ne tengo un capo; ma tu resti sola
né qui respiri nell'oscurità.

Oh l'orizzonte in fuga, dove s'accende
rara la luce della petroliera!
Il varco è qui? (Ripullula il frangente
ancora sulla balza che scoscende...).
Tu non ricordi la casa di questa
mia sera. Ed io non so chi va e chi resta.

[1930]

BEN JOHNSON (*fl.* 1950s/1960s) and
JAMES MERRILL (1926–95)

Johnson is the son of a prominent lawyer in Boston. He went to Rome as a Fulbright fellow and later was Lecturer at the University of Rome. He has published translations of stories by Svevo, Pavese, and Calvino, and *The Day of the Lion* (1954) and *Original Sin* (1956), novels by Giose Rimanelli. He also edited *Stories of Modern Italy* (1960).

Merrill was born in New York City and attended Amherst College. He first heard of Montale from Irma Brandeis when they were colleagues at Bard College in 1946. In an interview with Donald Sheehan in 1967, he said that in translating Montale's poems he "felt close to the feeling behind" them, which he described as "emotional refinement, gloomy and strongly curbed." Merrill was the first translator whose powers in English approximated Montale's powers in Italian. He met Johnson shortly after arriving in Rome in the spring of 1950 and gives a brief account of their collaboration in his memoir, *A Different Person* (1993). Merrill's books of poems include *The Changing Light At Sandover* (1982) and *Late Settings* (1985).

The House of the Customs Men

You do not remember the house of the customs men
above the cliff-face on a lurching rise:
desolate, it awaits you since the evening when
your thoughts swarmed in,
there restlessly to pause.

For years the libeccio has lashed the old walls
and the sound of your laughter is no longer gay:
the compass spins haphazard, the dice-score
adds up no longer. You do not remember;

another time distracts your memory;
a strand is drawn back into the skein.

I still have hold of an end; but the house recedes
and high upon the roof the weathercock
smokeblacked keeps revolving mercilessly.
I have hold of an end; but you remain alone
nor here do you breathe in the dark.

O fleeing horizon, where but rarely shine
lights of the tanker! Is the passage here?
(Breakers still spring against the plunging cliff...)
You do not remember the house of this evening of mine.
And I do not know who goes and who remains.

1952

ROBERT LOWELL

The Coastguard House

A death-cell? The shack of the coastguards
is a box over the drop to the breakers;
it waits for you without an owner,
ever since the mob of your thoughts
bullied a welcome,
and stayed on there, unrequited.
You didn't take it to heart.

For years the sirocco gunned the dead stucco with sand;
the sound of your laugh is a jagged coughing;
the compass, a pin-head, spins at random;
the dizzy dice screw up the odds.
You haven't taken my possession to heart;
another time has thinned your nostalgia;
a thread peels from the spool.

I hold an end of it,
but the house balks backward;
its sea-green weathercock
creaks and caws without pity.
I keep one end of the thread,
but you house alone
and hold your hollow breath there in the dark.

Oh the derelict horizon,
sunless except for the
orange hull of a lonely, drudging tanker!
The breakers bubble on the dead-drop.
You haven't taken my one night's possession to heart;
I have no way of knowing
who forces an entrance.

1961

JEREMY REED

The Coastguard's House

You don't recall the coastguard's house, that lair
perched like a crow's-nest so precariously
above the sheer rock-fall to the breakers,
that hung there as a desolate shelter
for the mad torrent of your thoughts to hive
in, restless, unrequited.

For years the sirocco's whipped paint to shale,
and the sound of your laughter is a gale
that spins the maddened compass needle aimlessly
as the wrong throw of dice your words turn up.
You won't recall; a sea-blur hangs over
your memory; a thread unwinds.

I hold an end of it, but the rocked house
recedes; the sea-warped weathervane clatters,
and wind ferociously snaps at pennants.
I keep my thread, fishing for you who cower
alone there, breathless in the spinning dark.

On the shifting horizon a tanker's
red light flickers right out on the edge...
Is this the crossing of our threads where surf
seethes in its boiling-pot beneath the cliff?
You don't remember our jagged outpost,
or which of us remains, and which goes lost.

1990

JONATHAN GALASSI

The House of the Customs Men

You don't recall the house of the customs men
high on the bluff that drops sheer to the reef:
it's been waiting, deserted, since the evening
your thoughts swarmed in
and hovered, nervously.

Sou'westers have lashed the old walls for years
and your laugh's not carefree anymore:
the compass needle staggers crazily
and the dice no longer tell the score.
You don't remember: other times
assail your memory; a thread gets wound.

I hold one end still; but the house recedes
and the smoke-stained weathervane
spins pitiless up on the roof.
I have one end; but you're alone,
not here, not breathing in the dark.

Oh the vanishing horizon line,
where the tanker's light shines faint!
Is the channel here? (The breakers
still seethe against the cliff that drops away...)
You don't recall the house of this, my evening.
And I don't know who's going or who'll stay.

2000

EDWIN MORGAN

Low Tide

Evenings alive with cries, the garden swing
Flashing in the arbour of those days
And a dark veil of mist hardly hiding
The sea's fixed face.

All past, all gone. Rapid slanting flights
Cross the wall now, and the crumbling, the fall
Of all things without respite is a confusion
Burdening the steep bank, burdening the rock
That first bore you on the ocean.

Now I am brought with the light breath of spring
A ghostly eddying
Of the drowned swallowed times and lives; and at evening,
Dusky convolvulus, only your memory
Twines, and wards off time.

It climbs on the parapet, on the tunnel in the distance
Where the slow slow train crawls into its lair.
Then comes a sudden gathering on the hillsides,
The flock of the moon, invisibly browsing there.

1959

W. S. DI PIERO (b. 1945)

Di Piero is the author of several books of poems, most recently, *Skirts and Slacks* (2001), and two collections of essays, *Memory and Enthusiasm: Essays 1975–1985* (1989) and *Out of Eden: Essays on Modern Art* (1991). His translations from Italian are Leopardi's *Pensieri* (1981), *This Strange Joy: The Collected Poems of Sandro Penna* (1982), and *The Ellipse: Selected Poems of Leonardo Sinisgalli* (1983). He has taught at Stanford since 1982. His poems in this volume appear in print for the first time.

Stanzas

I still can't find the source
of the blood you're nourished by,
endless rings eddied beyond
this brief arc of human days,
which delivered you to a present
of shrieked agony you've never known,
in this stinking bottomless swamp
of a star; now it's lymph that roughs out
your hands, flutters your pulse and, unseen,
enflames or blanches your image.

Yet the little webbing of your nerves
traces the memory of that journey,
and when I unveil your eyes they burn
with passion veiled by a crest
of restless sea foam that clenches
then shatters, and in your roaring temples
you hear it hiss away into your life,
the way a silent drowsy piazza
wakens with the boomed clap
of doves taking flight.

You're unaware of the sunburst rays
that converge in you; some appeared, of course,
to others: to the man who shivered one night
jolted by a fugitive white wing;
to the one who saw wandering shades where
others saw swarms of little girls
or who saw in the clear sky
a crack like forked lightning and
the world's clanging watch works,
revealed where the sky ripped open,
enraptured him, wailing.

In you I see a last corolla
of weightless ash that doesn't last
but scatters and falls. Willed
unwilled – such is your nature.
You touch the sign then pass over. O
plucked bow thrumming, furrow that rends
the sea swell then seals it up! And now
the last bubble rises high. Maybe
damnation is the bitter raving half-dark
that falls upon the one who stays behind.

JEREMY REED

Mesco Point

At dawn, unbending flights of partridges
skimmed over the quarry's skyline,
the smoke from explosives lazily puffed
in eddies up the blind rockface. The ridge
brightened. The trail of foam left by the pilot boat's
beaked prow settled into illusory
white flowers on the surface of the sea.

I still recall the path down here I tracked
once like a troubled dog. The swell pitches
between rocks and the backwash cargoes straw.
Nothing's changed, the wet gravel's still shaken
by detonations; the hunched stonebreakers
bend and huddle from the wind.

The bleak landscape brings back something of you.
A pneumatic drill gouges into rock
and smashes granite. A smoke flare goes up:
I smart, and redefine with clarity
your rare features, now they return to me,
jerky, imprecise, for a moment there,
then blasted by the next charge into air.

1990

JONATHAN GALASSI

Punta del Mesco

In the sky above the quarry, scored at dawn
by the plumb-line flight of partridges,
smoke from the mines was slowly thinning,
climbing the sheer cliffs.
Silent bugling naiads dove
from the stern of the pilot boat and quickly
drowned in the foam
your footsteps used to trace.

I see the path I ran along one day
like a nervous dog; it laps the stream,
rises among the rocks where wisps of straw
keep hiding it. And nothing's changed.
The washed gravel rumbles,
echoing the roar. The sun shines wet
on the tired stonecutters' backs
hunkered over their hammers.

Figureheads that resurface and bring me
something of you. A drill etches
the heart on rock – a louder blast
explodes around. I grope in smoke,
but see again: your few gestures come alive
and the face that dawns at the windowsill –
your childhood shattered by gunfire
lives again!

2000

ROBIN FULTON (b. 1937)

Born on the Isle of Arran, Scotland, and educated at Edinburgh University, Fulton has taught English since 1973 at Stavanger College, Norway. A prodigious translator of Scandinavian literature, he received the Swedish Academy's award for translation in 1978. His Italian translations appear in *An Italian Quartet: Versions after Saba, Ungaretti, Montale, and Quasimodo* (1966).

Summer

The kestrel throws a dark sign of the cross
on saplings patiently taking a grip on life.
And the cloud that has a cloud's-eye view?
Too many faces trickle from the spring.

In his feud with the current the trout tosses
rainbow hoops and flicks through them
and here perhaps even you, dead
Arethusa, come to pause in my steps.

Look at the livid shoulders, the dull nugget
turned over to show its glint in the sun,
the delirious cabbage-white, the spider's
impossible bridge across the torrent –

and something is going its own way and much
else that will not go through the eye of a needle;

to make even one life, too
many other lives have to touch.

1966

ROBERT LOWELL

Eastbourne

"*God save the king,*" the trumpets bray
from a pavilion laid on stilts,
leaving a freeway for the tide
to rise and sweep the horses's hoof-prints,
still legible in the wet sand.
A cold wind strikes against me, but
a glimmer burns the windows, the cliffs'
white mica glitters in that glare –
Bank Holiday ... It's bringing back
the long gliding wave of my life,
too pleasant in its downward fall.
It gets late, and the brassy noise
balloons, then sags in silence, dies.
On wheelchairs the disabled pass,
escorted by their long-eared dogs,
old parents, tongue-tied children. (And
tomorrow this will seem a dream.)
And you come, prisoner voice, you too,
released soul that has wandered far,
the blood's voice, lost and given back
tonight. A turning hotel door
shows its lit lobby, another door
turns, flashes back its answering ray;
a carousel arouses me,
spinning everything on its wheel;
and I, intent on hearing you
("*my country*"), recognize your breathing;
I too rise up, the day is far
too crowded. Everything is vain:
even the force that in its whirlwind

picks up the dead and living, rocks
and trees, in you, for you, evolving.
The holiday has no pity.
Again the band crashes its brass.
In the first dusk, a goodness, without
ties or armament, unfolds.
Evil wins ... The wheel does not stop.
Light-in-darkness, you knew this too,
and on the burning sky-line, where
you vanished at the bell's first call,
only the charred black brand is left
of what was once *Bank Holiday*.

c. 1960

BEN JOHNSON and
JAMES MERRILL

New Stanzas

Now that the last shreds of tobacco
die at your gesture in the crystal bowl,
to the ceiling slowly
rises a spiral of smoke
which the chess knights and chess bishops
regard bemused; which new rings follow,
more mobile than those
upon your fingers.

The mirage, that in the sky released
towers and bridges, disappeared
at the first puff; the unseen window
opens and the smoke tosses. Down below
another swarming: a horde
of men who do not know this incense of yours,
on the chessboard whose meaning you
alone compose.

My doubt was once that you perhaps ignored
yourself the game that on the board
evolves and now is storm cloud at your doors.
Death's frenzy (for you inciting
the god of chance, when he helps) subsides at no
small cost, if small be the flame in your gaze,
but, past the close-meshed curtains, asks
a further blaze.

Today I know what you want; la Martinella
tolls faintly and frightens
the ivory figures in a spectral
snowfield light. But he resists and is
rewarded for the lonely vigil
who can with you, to this burning glass
that blinds the pawns, oppose
your eyes of steel.

1956

EDWIN MORGAN

New Stanzas

Now with a gesture you put out the last
Glowings of tobacco in the crystal dish,
And now the smoke in a slow spiral winds,
Climbs to the ceiling
And hovers over the blank gaze of the chessmen,
The knights and bishops; and now ring after ring
Mounts up, more living than the clinging
Rings on your fingers.

Vanished the fata morgana, the bridges of mirage,
Towers flung to the clouds –
At the first puff, gone; the smoke is shaken,
A window opens unseen. But look down there:
Phantom multitudes of a different world,
Throngs of men to whom this incense of yours
Is nothing, a chessboard world whose very meaning
Is yours to compose.

There was a time when I doubted what you knew:
Maybe as the game unfolded on that square
You moved elsewhere – though now it lours at your door:
The frenzy of extinction is not calmed
At a cheap price, if the flash of your eyes is brief,
But cries for other fires, beyond the smokescreen
The god of chance throws thickly up for you
When he is on your side.

Today I know what you want; I hear the stroke
Of Martinella, and the hoarse bell sends
Its fear to chill the ivory spines in a light
As ghostly as the snow-glare. But to endure:
To win the reward of a lonely vigil: this still
Belongs to whoever with you can cast, strong
Against the burning-glass that blinds the pawns,
Your gaze of steel.

1959

EDITH FARNSWORTH

The Return*

Bocca di Magra

Here are the southwesterly and the mist
over the lapping sand dunes
and there, concealed by the uncertain cloud
or tossed by the to-and-fro of the foam,
is Duilio, the boatman who is crossing,
straining at his oars; here is
the terser allspice of the pines spreading
among poplars and young willows,
and the flailing windmills, and the footpath
wandering with the wave into the muddy creek,
the poisonous fungating morula; here, still,
are the dilapidated circular steps
meandering down beyond the verandah
in a frozen polychrome of joists,
there it is, listening to you, our old
staircase, vibrating to your voice when, saraband,
you gaily laughed from out the music box,
or when cold Furies blow infernal serpents
and the last shouts die away
upon the shores; and here is the sun
which finishes its course and drops from sight
within the margins of the song – here is
your dark tarantulan bite: I am prepared.

1970

*Aria, in which the Mozartian "Snakes of Hell" may not entirely account for
the final storm. [Author's note.]

DAVID FERRY

News from Mount Amiata

By later tonight the fireworks of the storm
Will be a swarming of bees below the horizon.
I'm writing this letter to you at a wooden table
Whose wood the insects and worms have gotten into.
The beams are pockmarked with their ravenous feasting.
A smell of melon mildew rises from the floor,
As from the valley rises the valley smoke,
As it were the smoke of mushrooms, clouding my window.
Here in the rich core of the world, in this room,
In this honeycomb, mealy, fragrant, innermost cell
Of a sphere launched out across the luminous skies,
You who are elsewhere and other dwell in another
Cell and center of things, but, here at this table,
Writing to you, in front of this fire the chestnuts
Lavishly burst themselves open upon the hearth of,
That life is too brief that invokes your absent presence
Against the glowing background as of an icon.

Outside the windows the rain is falling...
                                        If you
Were to make your way among the ancient feeble
Soot-blackened buildings time has made that way,
And along the alleys between them, and through the
        courtyards
Where in the middle there is a wellhead where
The well goes down forever and forever,

If you could follow the heavy flights of nightbirds
Down the alleys to where, beyond the ravine,
The galaxy glimmers, the matrix of our torment...
But the only step that echoes along the darkness
Is that of someone by himself who sees
Shadows of doorways falling, shadows collapsing;
The threads between the stars are lost to sight;
The clock in the campanile is stopped at two;
Even the vines that climb the ancient walls
Are shadows that climb in the dark.

                          North Wind, come down,
Unloosen the hands that clutch the sandstone walls;
Scatter the books of hours on the attic floors.
Clear all away, cold wind, and then, let all
Be clearness of sight that has dominion over
The mind that does not know how to despair.
Cold wind, seal up the spores from which the tendrils
Sprout that then climb as shadows the ancient walls.
These alleys are too narrow; the donkey hooves
That clatter in the darkness on the cobbles
Strike sparks the unseen mountain peak above
Replies to with magnesium random signals;
And oh the leaking slowly deliquescing
Walls of the huddled houses in the rain,
Time turning to water, the endless dialogue
With the wretched dead, the ashes, oh, the wind,
The death, the death that lives ....

                            This Christian fuss –
Nothing but words of shadow and of grief –
What can I say through them that speaks to you?
Less than the water draining away down the runnels.

An old abandoned mill wheel, the trunk of a tree,
Markers of the limits of the world...
A pile of litter shakes and disintegrates...
At night the porcupines come out, seeking
A trickle of water to pity them ... They join
My waking vigil to your deep dreaming sleep.

1999

LA BUFERA E ALTRO

The Storm and Other Poems

1956

CHARLES GUENTHER (b. 1920)

Guenther is a poet, translator, reviewer, editor, and librarian who has lived steadily in St Louis. In 1973 he was awarded the Order of Merit of the Italian Republic for his translations of Italian poets. These appear in *Modern Italian Poets* (1961) and *The Hippopotamus: Selected Translations 1945–1985* (1986). Montale's title for the following poem is "Lungomare," a seaside promendade.

Seascape

The wind rises, the dark is torn to shreds,
and the shadow you cast on the fragile
railing bristles. Too late

if you want to be yourself! The mouse
drops from the palm tree, the lightning's on the fuse,
on the long, long lashes of your gaze.

1975

ROBERT BLY (b. 1926)

Bly is a poet, translator, editor, and lecturer. *The Eight Steps of Translation* (1983) offers a view of his practice as a translator. Among his many books is *Eating the Honey of Words: New and Selected Poems* (1999).

On a Letter Not Written

For a flock of daybreaks, for a few threads
on which the fleece of life is snarled
and then wound out
into hours and years – is it for this the dolphins in twos
are sporting today with their children? Oh that I could hear
    from you
nothing at all, and that I could escape from the ghostly lights
of your eyelashes. Surely there is something else on earth.

I cannot disappear or come forward. The red furnace
of night is late
coming, the evening goes on,
prayer is torture, and not yet among the rocks
that are rising have you received
the bottle from the sea. The empty wave
breaks on the point, at Land's End.

1962

ALLEN MANDELBAUM

In Sleep

The song of screech-owls when an iris
fades with intermittent throbs,
the groans and sighs of youth, the error
that girds the temples, and the vague horror
of cedars staggered by the shock
of night – all this can still return
to me, can flood from ditches, burst
from dykes, alert me to your voice.
The sound of a cruel hurdy-gurdy
stings. The adversary clamps
his visor. The moon of amaranth
invades closed eyes; it is a cloud
that swells; and when sleep bears it deeper,
it is still, beyond death, blood.

2002

RACHEL WETZSTEON (b. 1967)

Wetzsteon studied at Yale, Johns Hopkins, and Columbia. She has published two books, *The Other Stars* (1994) and *Home and Away* (1998). This adaptation of "Nel sonno" was published in *Raritan*.

The violent thrum of error,
the catcalls of the wronged, the small
crimes of a life, and the liquid horror
of crimes to come – all
this gushes and spurts inside
me even in sleep, issuing from a source
I cannot stop anymore. But now, astride
a white-winged, metal horse,
you float above the sea, the dream
takes shape and lets you loom large ... until a cruel moon
spotlights the beast's false joints, and screams
blast it to shreds, and you come crashing down
into the red-hot waves. Even in sleep
I cannot save you from the carnal deep.

1994

GEORGE KAY

Indian Serenade

Ours, too, is the melting of the evening hour.
And for us, the streak that rises from the sea
to the park and wounds the aloes, too.

You can lead me by the hand, if you pretend
to believe you're here with me, if I'm fool enough
to follow you away and what you press,

what you say, to me seems in your power.
*
Were your life the one that holds me
upon the verge – and I could lend you a face,
rave you a shape. But it isn't, isn't true.

The polyp that insinuates
inky tentacles between the rocks
can make use of you. You belong to him

and don't know it. You're he and you think you're you.

1964

EDITH FARNSWORTH

The Earrings

The soot upon the mirror retains
no shade of flights. (Of yours no trace remains.)
Unopposed, the moving sponge blots out
the helpless glimmerings from the golden ring.
For you I sought your stones, the corals,
the strong seductive realm: I shun
the disincarnate goddess; desires for you I bear
until the time of their consumption in your light.
The dragonflies drone outside, the mad dirge
drones, knowing that two lives can hardly count.
Flaccid medusae of the night emerge,
returning to the setting. Your imprint
from below will come: where to your lobes
bleak upturned hands will fix the coral rings.

1970

EDITH FARNSWORTH

Window of Fiesole

Here where the furtive cricket gnaws
the garments of plant silk
and the scent of camphor hardly draws
away the moths that leave powder in the books,
the fledgling bird is clambering up the elm
in spirals and by the fronds the sun
is caught in shade. Another light
and other flames, which do not fulfill,
my scarlet ivy.

1970

EDITH FARNSWORTH

The Ark

The spring storm has turned inside out
the umbrella of the willow,
the April gale has snared
within the yard that golden fleece
which hides my dead,
my trusted dogs, my old
attendants – from that day on, how many
(when the willow was blond and with my sling
I cut away the locks) have fallen
panting into the trap. Certainly
the storm will reunite them all beneath
that former roof, but farther off, much farther
from this fulgurated ground where
blood and lime are boiling in the imprint
of the human foot. The ladle is smoking
in the kitchen, its circle of reflections
frames the bony faces, the pointed
muzzles, sheltered by the magnolia
in the background, if a breath should
blow her there. With a howl
of loyalty the spring storm shakes
my ark, oh my lost ones.

1970

JEREMY REED

Day and Night

Even a feather floating in the air
can sketch your figure, or the blue sunbeam
skirting the furniture, the reflection
of a child's mirror flashed from a roof-top.
On the circuit of walls, vaporous steam
elongates the needling poplars,
and the knife-grinder's parrot down below
is a green temper of ruffled plumage
on a trestle. The stifling night
drops on the square; footsteps reverberate.
It's hard this breathless struggle, going down
to rise again from a nightmare that lasts
centuries, or moments, and win back
the light of your eyes in the glowing cave.
Now it begins, the agonised
cries of someone drawn to a balcony...
And it could still happen, a sudden shot
ring out, reddening the throat and shattered wings
of the dawn's dangerous and inimical messenger,
and the cloisters and hospitals wake
to the strident brass of trumpets...

1990

EAMON GRENNAN

To My Mother

Now that the chorus of quails
lulls you to eternal sleep, a scattered
flock in light-hearted flight
towards the high, harvested headland
of Cape Mesco; now that the war of the living
grows more ferocious,
if you lay your body by like a shade

                                 (and it isn't a shade,
dear heart, it's not what you think),

who will look after you? The empty street
is a dead end: only two hands, a face,
those hands, *that* face, the gesture
of a life nothing else but itself –
only this will bring you
to the paradise thronged with souls and voices
in which you live,

and the question you leave, this too
a gesture of yours, in the shadow of the crosses.

EDITH FARNSWORTH

From a Tower

I have seen the white-winged sparrow
spring from the lightning rod:
by his disdainful flight I knew him,
and by his flute roulade.

I have seen the gay, long-eared
Piquillo bound from the mausoleum,
and clamber up a humid chute
of steps to reach his home.

In window panes of stained glass
I have seen a land of skeletons pass
through flowers in bifore – and one
lip of blood become more mute.

1970

CHARLES WRIGHT

Where the Tennis Court Was...

Where the tennis court once was, enclosed by the small rectangle down by the railroad tracks where the wild pines grow, the couch-weed now runs matted over the ground, and the rabbits scratch in the tall grass in those hours when it is safe to come out.

One day here two sisters came to play, two white butterflies, in the early hours of the afternoon. Toward the east the view was (and still is) open – and the damp rocks of the Corone still ripen the strong grapes for the "*sciacchetra.*" It is curious to think that each of us has a country like this one, even if altogether different, which must always remain *his* landscape, unchanging; it is curious that the physical order of things is so slow to filter down into us, and then so impossible to drain back out. But what of the rest? Actually, to ask the how and why of the interrupted game is like asking the how and why of that scarf of vapor rising from the loaded cargo ship anchored down there at the docks of Palmaria. Soon they will light, in the gulf, the first lamps.

Around, as far as the eye can see, the iniquity of objects persists, intangibly. The grotto encrusted with shells should be unchanged in the dense and heavy-planted garden under the tennis court; but the fanatical uncle will come no more with his tripod camera and magnesium lamp to photograph the single flower, unrepeatable, risen from the spiny cactus, and predestined to live only the shortest of lives. Even the villas of the South Americans seem deserted. And there haven't always been the heirs and heiresses ready to squander their sumptuously shoddy goods that came always side-by-side with the rattle of pesos and milreis. Or maybe the sarabande of the newly arrived tells us of passings on to other regions: surely we here are perfectly sheltered and out of the line of fire. It is almost as though life could not be ignited here except by lightning; as though it feeds only on such inert things as it can safely accumulate; as though it quickly cankers in such deserted zones.

"*Del salon en el angulo oscuro – silenciosa y cubierta de polvo – veiase el arpa...*" Oh, yes, the museum would be impressive if one were able to uncover this ex-paradise of Victoriana. And no one was ever seen again on the seashell-inlayed terrace, supported by the giant Neptune (now scraped clean) after the Lion of Callao lost the election, and died; but there, by the outrageous bay window, frescoed in pears, apples and the serpents of the earthly paradise, the good-hearted Señora Paquita thought, in vain, to carry out her serene old age, comforted by her wily needles and the smile of posterity. But one day the husbands of the daughters arrived (Brazilian sons-in-law), and, the mask having been ripped away, carried those good things off. Of the duenna, and of the others, not a word more was ever heard – one of the descendants came back later in one of the last wars and performed miracles, it is said. By then, however, it was, more or less, the time of the Tripolitan hymns. And these objects, these houses, stayed inside the living circle so long as it lasted. For few felt from the start that the cold was actually coming; and among these, perhaps, was my father who, even during the hottest days of August, supper out on the terrace over (carried on amidst moths and more persistent insects), and after having thrown a wool shawl around his shoulders, would repeat, always in French for who knows what reason, "*il fait bien froid, bien froid*"; then he would go off immediately into his room and lie down on the bed and smoke his 7 centime Cavour.

1978

WILLIAM ARROWSMITH

Visit to Fadin

On past Madonna dell'Orto, then a short walk under the porticoes in the center, and I turned up the ramp leading to the hospital, quickly making my way to the sick man taking the sun on the balcony with the other terminal cases. He wasn't expecting to see me. He recognized me immediately, showing no surprise. His hair, recently cut, was as usual extremely short, his face hollower and flushed at the cheekbones. His eyes were as beautiful as ever, but they had melted into a deeper halo. I arrived without warning, and on the wrong day; even his Carlina, "the angel musician," was unable to be with him.

Below us the sea was empty, and along the shore we could see the scattered marzipan architectures of the rich.

Last stop on the journey: some of your occasional companions (workingmen, clerks, hairdressers) had already preceded you, vanishing from their cots without a sound. You had brought several bundles of books with you and set them where you used to keep your knapsack: old books, old-fashioned books, except for a slender volume of poems which I took with me, and which I'll keep, as we both wordlessly surmised.

Of the conversation I remember nothing. Obviously there was no need for him to bring up the ultimate questions, the universal ones – he who had always lived in a human way, quietly and simply. Exit Fadin. And to say that you're no longer here is only to say that you've entered a different order, in that the order in which we loiterers move about, crazy as it is, seems to our way of thinking the only one in which divinity reveals its attributes, is recognized and savored, in the context of a task we don't understand. (Might even that divinity have need of us? If that's blasphemy, alas, it's by no means our worst.)

Always to be among the first, and to *know*, this is what matters, even if the *why* of the performance escapes us. The man who has had from you this high teaching of *daily decency* (the hardest of the virtues) can wait patiently for the book of your relics. Your word was not perhaps of the written kind.

1985

RACHEL WETZSTEON

This is an adaptation of "Di un natale metropolitano" ("A Metropolitan Christmas"). Montale specifies after his title that the city is London.

Mistletoe, a city of snapshots taped to
plaster, blue bottles and a fire's
fitful sparks the only glimmers
of warmth in your new lodgings.
For you, this season without wreaths,
I would manhandle a city, conjure
a drizzle, then soften it to snow,
paint lampposts deep reds and greens
and so install around your room some
snatches of the festive. But starting
and ending here, these wishes are slipshod:
they never seem to settle on a picture that
touches you at all. Storms, ramshackle
gifts fly freely, but the setting's
the same: you dine upon sausage and frost.

1994

G. SINGH (b. 1926)

Singh was born in Jaipur, India. He has degrees from the universities of Rajasthan, Bologna, and London, and since 1965 has taught Italian at Queen's University, Belfast. Between 1970 and 1980 he published the first book-length study in any language of Montale's poetry, edited a selection of his poems, and translated two of his books of poems, *New Poems* (1976) and *It Depends: A Poet's Notebook* (1980), a selection of his essays, and his volume of stories, *The Butterfly of Dinard* (1970; American edition 1971) – a decade of labor for which readers of Montale in English must be grateful.

Winter Light

When I stepped down from Palmira's
sky to the pygmy palms
and candied gateways and you scratched
my throat with your nails to warn me
that you were going to ravish me;
when I came down from the acropolis' sky
and saw miles and miles of baskets
full of octopuses and eels
(oh the sawing of those teeth on the benumbed
heart!), when I took leave of the peaks
of the inhuman auroras to enter
the icy museums of mummies
and scarabs (oh how you suffered,
my only life!) and compared
pumice with jasper, sand
with the sun, and mud with divine clay –
it was then that the spark went off
and I was burnt to ashes, renewed.

1972

JEREMY REED

Homage to Rimbaud

Emerging from her fragile chrysalis
a brilliant butterfly patrols the desk
of the recurrent exile from Charleville.
His flight was that of an arrowed partridge,
its feathers singed by marksmen.
Gardenias glint in the asphalt's black ice.
The butterfly touches a silk pollen
beneath the sun's scarlet halo.
He's elsewhere now, returned to the first source.
He owns the sky; his angel guards the bridge.

1990

JONATHAN GALASSI

Iris

When suddenly Saint Martin shunts his embers
down his sluiceway, stirring them
deep in Lake Ontario's dark furnace,
the popping of green pinecones in the ashes,
or the steam from a fume of poppies
and the bloodied Face on the shroud
that keeps me from you;

this and little else (if a sign,
a wink from you is little, in the struggle
that shoves me in a charnelhouse, back to the wall,
where sky-blue sapphires and palms
and storks aloft on one leg
can't hide the atrocious view
from the poor dismayed Nestorian);

this is all of you that reaches me
from the shipwreck of my people,
and yours, now an icy fire
recalls the land of yours you didn't see;
and I hold no other rosary in my hand,
no other flame than this of resin and berries
has given you form.

*

Another's heart is not your heart,
the lynx is nothing like the lovely tabby
stalking the hummingbird up in the laurel,
but they're the same to you, if you step out

beyond the shadow of the sycamore,
or else is it that mask on the white cloth,
the purple effigy that guided you?

So that your work (which is a form
of His) might flourish in other lights,
Iris of Canaan, you deliquesced
into that halo of mistletoe and holly
which bears your heart into the night
of the world, beyond the mirage
of the desert flowers, your kin.

If you appear, you bring me here again,
under the pergola of barren vines
by the landing on our river – and the ferry's not returning,
the Indian summer sun dissolves, goes black.
But if you come back, you're not you,
your earthly history is changed,
you don't wait for the prow at the pier,

you watch for nothing: yesterday or tomorrow;

for His work (which is transforming
into yours) *has to continue.*

2000

EAMON GRENNAN

In the Greenhouse

Everywhere among the lemon trees
the toddle-tipping skitter of moles;
the scythe glittered, dripping
a rosary of discreet droplets.

On the skin of each quince glinted
a single spark, the cochineal;
I could hear the pony bridling
under the comb – then the dream took over.

Ravished, light-headed, I was soaked
in you, the shape of you
my secret breath, your face
melting in mine – and on the few

who were alive, the dark
thought of God came down in a cloud
of heavenly noise, toy drums,
dangle-spheres of flashing light

on me, on you, on the lemon trees.

CHARLES WRIGHT

Beach at Versilia

I pray for my dead so that they might pray
for me, for my living, as I ask for them
not resurrection but, instead, the fulfillment
of that life they have had
unexplained, and unexplainable; today,
they rarely descend from the open horizons
when riots of water and sky open
windows to the tentacles of the evening – less and less often
a cutter, the sky-hung goshawk, white-crested,
white-pinioned, brings them to the sand.
Beds of zinnias dyed like wax flowers
(grandmothers with stiff, chin-strapped bonnets water them,
refusing to glance at anyone from the outside street
who won't surrender his sickness
into their unpitying hands); courtyards of grizzled, trellised
vines where angry voices
forbid left-overs to the friar-colored cat
if he dare enter; rubble and flat overlooks
on low houses along an undulating
descent of dunes, and umbrellas opened
against a grey sun; sand that can't nourish
the trees sacred to my childhood, the wild pine,
the fig and the eucalyptus.

In that shade my early years were crowded,
heavy with honey, so long abandoned;
in that shade, often spread out under
only two strips of crepe-paper riddled
with mosquitos, I slept – there, in the corner room,
next to the kitchen, at nighttime;

in the deeps of siestas
while cicadas jangled, dazzling in my sleep,
I sometimes would catch a glimpse, over the wall, at the
     wash-basin,
of the shadows of loved ones massaging the moray eels,
forcing the bones back to the tails, then cutting them out;
in that endless high humming
others now gone, with rakes and shears
would leave the nursery
of dwarf stalks for the burnt
evergreens, for the channels greedy for water.

Those years of cliffs and closed horizons
were custodians of lives still human,
of acts still understandable – like the breathing,
like the final sigh of underwater creatures
then similar to man, or close to him
even in name: the priest fish, the swallow fish,
the lobster – wolf of the trap – who
forgets his pinchers when Alice
comes near ... and the trapeze acts
of familiar mice from one palm tree
to the other – time that once was measurable
until this endless sea opened,
this sea of clay and washed-up refuse.

1978

BERNARD WALL (b. 1908)

Wall was educated at Stonyhurst College, the oldest Jesuit founda-
tion in England and the earliest Catholic public school, and at
Brasenose, Oxford, where he made common cause with a Catholic
coterie – Douglas Woodruff, Eric Gill, Ronald Knox, and Evelyn
Waugh. In 1939 he went to Rome on a mission to "convert the
Germans to peaceful and free ways of thinking by means of clandes-
tine posted communications" (*Headlong into Change*, 1969 – Wall's
autobiography). Nine months later he fled the Germans, but returned
to Rome in the wake of the Allied invasion of Sicily. After the war
he worked as editor of the journals *Colosseum, Changing World,*
and *Twentieth Century*. In the second of these he printed his first
Montale translations, although the following poem was published
in *Arena*, a Communist journal edited by Jack Lindsay. Wall has
written several books about Italy, notably *Italian Art, Life and Land-
scape* (1956) and *The Vatican Story* (1957).

Hitler Spring

And she to see whom all the heavens turn
          (Dante (?) to Giovanni Querini)

Thickly the whitened cloud from the maddened moths
whirls round the pallid standards and on the embankments,
spreads on the ground a pall that crackles
like sugar underfoot: now imminent summer releases
the night frost that it knew
in the dead seasons' secret quarries
in the gardens that from Maiano come leaping down to
          these sandbeds.

Down the corso just now there passed a herald of hell
in flight through the cheering assassins, and a mystic gulf of
     fire
beflagged with crooked crosses took him and swallowed
     him,
the poor shops have been shuttered
inoffensive though they too were armed
with cannons and toys of war,
the butcher has put up his bars, the one who adorned
the snouts of goat kids he had slain with berries,
the solemnities of still bloodless myths of killers
have turned into a filthy morris-feast of flattened wings
of ghosts on the mudflats, and the water goes on gnawing
the banks and no man is any longer blameless.

Was all for nought then? – the Roman candles
that slowly whitened the horizon at San Giovanni
and the pledges and the long good byes
strong as a baptism in mournful expectation
of the horde (but a jewel shot the air distilling
on the ice and shorelands of your coasts
Tobits angels, the seven, the seed
of the future) and the heliotropes born
of your hands – burnt and sucked dry
by the pollen that crackles like fire
and stabs like a sleety wind...
                        Oh the wounded
spring is still festive if this death
freezes again in death. Once anew
look upward Clizia, it is your fate, you
who in all change preserve your love unchanged
until the blinded sun you bear within you

is dazzled in the Other or is confounded
with Him, for all. Perhaps the alarms and sirens
welcoming these monsters in the evening
of their witches sabbath are already mingling
with the sound unleashed from heaven, descending,
    conquering –
with a breath of dawn that may be manifest
for all, to-morrow, white but without wings
of horror in the burnt gravel of the south...

1949

ROBERT LOWELL

Hitlerian Spring

A dense white cold of maddened moths
swaggers past parapet and lamp,
shaking a sheet upon the earth,
crackling like sugar underfoot.
Now the new season –
the nearing summer liberates
the thaw and chill
from stoneyard, lumberyard and orchard,
wood tossed by the river to its banks.

(An infernal possessor
motorcycles down the Corso;
hurrahing stooges and a jangle
of hooked crosses absorb and swallow
him – a thunderhead of light!)

                    The old shop
windows are shuttered, poor and harmless,
though even these are armed with cannon
and toys of war. This spring, the butcher
locks his creaking iron curtain –
once he would hook two goat's-heads crowned
with holly berries on his door...
they were a kind of ritual for
those mild young killers, unaware
the blood they spilled had been transformed
to a sick mangle of crushed wings.
Here barnacles and old mortgages
keep chiselling at the river-piles –
and no one, ahi, now is blameless!

The sirens and the tolling bells...
For nothing, then? On Saint John's Day,
the stinking roman candles scour
the air. Once more, spring! Now the slow
farewell, as sad as Baptism,
the mournful vigil of the horde,
the head brought in upon a board,
now diamond powder blurs the air,
and shakes down ice – the sky is like
Tobias looking at the sky,
seeing the seven seraphs flame.
Light rays and seeds are drifting down
through pollen hissing into fire,
through crushed and crooked fingers,
through the sharpness of driving snow,
the sirens and the tolling bells...

Clizia,
April's reopened wound is raw!...

1961

JONATHAN GALASSI

Voice That Came with the Coots

Since the road traveled, if I look back, is longer
than the goat-path bringing me
to where we'll melt like wax,
and not the flowering rushes but verbena,
the blood of cemeteries, soothes the heart,
here you are, Father, out of the dark that held you,
upright in the glare,
no shawl or beret,
in the dull dawn rumble that announced
the miners' barges, half sunk with their cargo,
black on the high waves.

The shade that comes with me
and stands watch at your grave,
who sits on a herm and haughtily
tosses her childish bangs
to free her burning eyes and severe brow –
this shade weighs no more than yours
interred so long;
the day's first rays transfix her,
vivid butterflies dance through her,
and the sensitive mimosa
touches her and won't recoil.

The loyal shadow and the mute one
standing again; she whom inner fire
unbodied and the one long years out of time
(years for me in my heaviness) have unfleshed,
exchange words that I can't hear,
stiff at the sidelines; perhaps the first

will recover the form that burned with love
for Him who moved her, not self-love;
but the other quails, afraid that the ghost
of memory in which he is warm for his children
will be lost in this new leap.

"I've thought for you, I've remembered
for all. Now you return to the open
sky that transmutes you. Does this cliff
still tempt you? Yes, the high-water mark
is the same as ever, the sea
that linked you with my beaches before I had wings
hasn't dissolved. I remember them,
my shores, yet I've come with the coots
to take you from yours.
Memory is no sin while it avails.
After, it's molelike torpor, misery

that mushrooms on itself..."
                                        The wind of day
melds the living shadow
and the other, still reluctant one
in an amalgam that repels my hands,
and the breath breaks out of me at the swelling point,
in the moat that surrounds the release of memory.
So it reveals itself before attaching
to images, or words, dark reminiscent
sense, the unlived-in void we occupied
that waits for us until the time has come
to fill itself with us, to find us again...

2000

KEITH BOSLEY (b. 1937)

Bosley has translated poetry from the Finnish and French, notably *Tales from the Long Lakes: Finnish Legends from the Kalevala* (1966) and *Mallarmé: The Poems* (1977). He has also edited *The War Wife: Vietnamese Poetry* (1972) and *The Elek Book of Oriental Verse* (1979).

The Shadow of the Magnolia

The shadow of the Japanese magnolia
thins out now its purple buds
have fallen. High up, a cicada
whirrs fitfully. Gone is
the time of voices in unison,
Clizia, the time of the boundless god
who devours and puts new blood into his faithful.
Expense of self was easier, death
at the first wingbeat, at the first encounter
with the enemy, a game. Now
the harder way begins: but not for you, wasted
by the sun and rooted, just a downy
fieldfare flying high over the cold
wharves of your river – not for you, frail
refugee to whom zenith nadir cancer
capricorn were always much the same
for war to be in you and in who adores
the marks on you of your Bridegroom, the curling
shiver of frost ... The others draw back
and bend. The file that finely
cuts will be silent, the empty husk
of who sang will turn straight to powdered
glass underfoot, the shadow is blenched –

it is autumn, winter, it is the beyond
that leads you and into which I plunge, a mullet
high and dry at the new moon.

Goodbye.

1972

Il gallo cedrone

Dove t'abbatti dopo il breve sparo
(la tua voce ribolle, rossonero
salmì di cielo e terra a lento fuoco)
anch'io riparo, brucio anch'io nel fosso.

Chiede aiuto il singulto. Era più dolce
vivere che affondare in questo magma,
più facile disfarsi al vento che
qui nel limo, incrostati sulla fiamma.

Sento nel petto la tua piaga, sotto
un grumo d'ala; il mio pesante volo
tenta un muro e di noi solo rimane
qualche piuma sull'ilice brinata.

Zuffe di rostri, amori, nidi d'uova
marmorate, divine! Ora la gemma
delle piante perenni, come il bruco,
luccica al buio, Giove è sotterrato.

[1943]

BERNARD WALL

The Wood Grouse

Where you fall headlong with the brief burst of firing
(your cry ferments, red-black
broth of heaven and earth over slow coals)
I too take shelter, I too burn in the ditch.

The sob is a cry for help. It was sweeter
to be alive than sink into this lava,
easier to fall to pieces in the wind
than here in the mud, incrusted on the flame.

In your breast I feel your wound, beneath
a clot of wing; my dull and ponderous flight
attempts a wall and of us there remains
only some feathers on the frosted ilex.

Tussles of nests, loves, nests marbled
with eggs, ah godlike! now the jewel
of the perennial plants, like the caterpillar,
sparkles in the darkness, Jove is buried.

1974

WILLIAM ARROWSMITH

The Capercaillie

Where you went down after the shot was fired
(your voice comes boiling back up, black-red
salmi of earth and heaven, simmering),
there I too take shelter, I too burn in that ditch.

Pain cries for help. Living was sweeter
than sinking down in this magma,
simpler to dissolve in the wind than here
in this mud, scabbing over flame.

I feel your wound in my breast, beneath
a clot of wings; my lumbering flight
attempts a wall, and all that's left of us
is a few feathers on the frosted holly.

Scuffles over nests, matings, nests
of marbled, heavenly eggs! Now,
in darkness, the perennials' budded gem glitters
like the grub. Jove is underground.

1985

L'anguilla

L'anguilla, la sirena
dei mari freddi che lascia il Baltico
per giungere ai nostri mari,
ai nostri estuarî, ai fiumi
che risale in profondo, sotto la piena avversa,
di ramo in ramo e poi
di capello in capello, assottigliati,
sempre più addentro, sempre più nel cuore
del macigno, filtrando
tra gorielli di melma finché un giorno
una luce scoccata dai castagni
ne accende il guizzo in pozze d'acquamorta,
nei fossi che declinano
dai balzi d'Appennino alla Romagna;
l'anguilla, torcia, frusta,
freccia d'Amore in terra
che solo i nostri botri o i disseccati
ruscelli pirenaici riconducono
a paradisi di fecondazione;
l'anima verde che cerca
vita là dove solo
morde l'arsura e la desolazione,
la scintilla che dice
tutto comincia quando tutto pare
incarbonirsi, bronco seppellito;
l'iride breve, gemella
di quella che incastonano i tuoi cigli
e fai brillare intatta in mezzo ai figli
dell'uomo, immersi nel tuo fango, puoi tu
non crederla sorella?

[1948]

BEN JOHNSON and
JAMES MERRILL

The Eel

The eel, siren
of cold seas who leaves the Baltic
to come to our waters,
our estuaries, rivers
whose depths she swims, under the adverse flood,
from branch to branch, then
from vein to tapering vein,
ever more inward, ever more into the heart
of rock, filtering
through runnels of mud until one day
a light, darted from the chestnut-trees,
kindles a flashing in pits of stagnant water,
in ditches binding
cliffs of the Apennines to Romagna;
the eel, torch, whip,
arrow of Love on earth
whom only our gullies or the parched
Pyrenean brooks lead back
to the paradise of her spawning;
the green soul seeking
life where only
drought gnaws, and desolation,
the spark saying
all begins when all seems
to burn and blacken, an interred bole,

the tiny iris, twin
of the one you mount in the midst of your eyelashes
and make glisten untouched among the human
children, sunk in your slime, can you not
think her a sister?

1953

EDWIN MORGAN

The Eel

The eel, the sea siren
That leaves behind her cold Baltic waters
In order to sport in our seas,
Our river-mouths, our rivers
Which she ascends against the deep-borne tides,
From arm to arm of the streams
Narrowing from rill to rill,
Inward always, inward, on to the heart
Of stone, filtering through
The tiny channels of the mud until one day
A light struck from the chestnut-trees
Silvers a frisking in the standing pools
Of ditches running down
From the rocks of the Apennines to the Romagna;
The eel: the brand, the lash,
The shaft of Love on earth
That only our headlong gullies or the dried
Pyrenean brooks
Lead back to her teeming gardens;
The green desire that searches
For life where only drought
Clenches and the desert hardens,
The sap and spark that speak
Of a world in birth when all the world appears
Half carbonized, a buried stump-like bulk;

The brief rainbow, a twin
To that other iris set within your brows
Which you flash out unclouded on the crowds
Of the children of men plunged in your muds – can you
    doubt
It is your sister that swims in?

1959

KEVIN HART (b. 1954)

Hart is an Australian who grew up in London and Brisbane. He teaches now at Notre Dame. His books include *The Buried Harbour: Selected Poems of Giuseppe Ungaretti* (1990), *New and Selected Poems* (1995), and *Wicked Heat* (1999).

The Eel

The eel, the siren
of freezing waters, abandoning the Baltic
for our warm seas,
our estuaries and rivers, ascending
deeply against the water's force
from branch to branch, and then
from stream to stream, threading
ever inwards, ever deeper into the heart
of the rock, thrashing
through mud until one day
a light shot from the chestnut trees
catches its sparkle in pools of dead water,
in ditches streaming
down Appenine cliffs to the Romagna;
the eel, torch, lash,
arrow of Love on earth
led only by gullies, by dried-up mountain creeks
back to paradise;
the green soul seeking
life where only
drought and desolation feast,
the spark announcing
that all begins where all appears
burnt black, a buried stick;

quick rainbow, iris, twin
of her your eye sets on
shining, whole – here,
where men luxuriate in your mud, can you
not see her as your sister?

1979

VINIO ROSSI (b. 1924) and
DAVID YOUNG (b. 1936)

Rossi taught French and Italian at Oberlin College for many years. He has translated, with Stuart Friebert, *The Coldest Year of Grace: Selected Poems of Giovanni Raboni* (1985).

Young's books of poems include *The Planet on the Desk: Selected and New Poems 1960–1990* (1991). He has published three books on Shakespeare's plays and edits *Field*. The following untitled poem is the second of the "Madrigali Privati" ("Private Madrigals") that make up Part IV of *La bufera e altro*.

You gave my name to a tree? That's not much;
and I'm not resigned to remaining
a shadow or a trunk
abandoned in the suburbs. As for yours
I've given it to a river, to a long fire, to the crude
game of my luck, to the superhuman
faith with which you spoke to the toad
that came out of the sewer, without horror or pity
or exultation, to the breath of those strong
soft lips of yours that succeed,
by naming, in creating: toad flower grass reef –
oak ready to unfurl overhead
when the rain prunes the meaty
petals of the clover and the fire grows.

1980

BERNARD WALL

The Red and the Black

Magenta-colored clouds were thickening
on the Fingal's cave beyond the coast
when I said "pedal,
my darling" and with a leap
the tandem broke from the mud, was liberated
in flight amid the berries on the knoll.

Bronze-colored clouds were folding
bridgewise on the spirals of the Agliena
on the rusty whiteness, when
you said "stop" and your wing of ebony
filled up the horizon
with its long shudder, impossible to sustain.

Like Paphnutius in the desert I wished too much
to overcome you, I being overcome.
I fly with you, I stay with you; to die,
to live is one only point, a tempest dyed
with your color, warm with the breath
of the cavern, depth, scarcely audible.

1974

JONATHAN GALASSI

From a Swiss Lake

My vixen, I myself was once the "*poète*
Assassiné": there where the hazel grove,
Razored by a bonfire, makes a cave;
In that den
A sequined halo
Lit your face, then slowly fell
Until it touched a cloud, dissolved; and anxiously
I called for the end above that deep
Sign of your open, bitter life,
Abominably delicate, yet strong.

Shining in the darkness, is it you?
Plumbing that throbbing furrow, on
An incandescent path, hot in pursuit of your
Zombie predator pawprint (nearly
Invisible star-shaped trace),
A stranger, I plunge anew; and a black duck
Now rising from the bottom of the lake
Invites me to the new fire that will singe her.

2000

CHARLES WRIGHT

Anniversary

From the time of your birth,
little fox, I have been on my knees.
From that day on I have felt the war
with evil won, my sins atoned for.

A flame was burning and burning; onto your roof,
onto mine, I saw the terror overflow.
You grew like a young stalk; and I, in the coolness
of battle lulls, spied on that growing up.

I stay on my knees: the gift that I dreamed of,
not for me but for everyone,
belongs now only to me, with God divided
from men, from the blood clotted and crisp
on the high branches, on the fruit.

1978

EDWIN MORGAN

Brief Testament

This thing in the dark like a marsh-light
That flits through the vault of my head,
This snail-track shining like pearl,
This crushed-glass emery-gleam –
It is not the lamp of any church or workshop
Nourished by acolyte
Whether in black or in red.
Only this iris is mine
To leave you, the memorial
Of a faith that was often invaded,
Of a hope that burned more slowly
Than a stubborn log in the fire.
Keep its powder in the mirror
When every lamp goes out
And hell's sardana is danced
And a shadow-black Lucifer swoops down on a prow
In Thames or Hudson or Seine,
Flapping his tarry wings that are half
Torn off with exertion and effort, to tell you: Now!
Hardly a heritage – nor is it a mascot
For standing up to onslaughts from monsoons
On the mere spider's thread of memory –
But it is only in ashes that a story endures,
Nothing persists except extinguished things.
It was the sign all right: the one whose luck
Is to see it can never miss you again.

Each recognizes his own: the pride
Was not an escape, the humility was not
A meanness, the ghostly flash that was struck
Down there was not the spark of a match on a box.

1959

ROBERT LOWELL

Little Testament

This thing the night flashes
like marshlight through the skull of my mind,
this pearl necklace snail's trail,
this ground glass, diamond-dust sparkle –
it is not the lamp in any church or office,
tended by some adolescent altar boy,
Communist or papist,
in black or red.
I have only this rainbow
to leave you, this testimonial
of a faith, often invaded,
of a hope that burned more slowly
than a green log on the fire.
Keep its spectrum in your pocket-mirror,
when every lamp goes out,
when hell's orchestra trembles,
and the torch-bearing Lucifer
lands on some bowsprit
in the Thames, Hudson or Seine –
rotating his hard coal wings,
half lopped by fatigue, to tell you, "Now."
It's hardly an heirloom or charm
that can tranquillize monsoons
with the transparent spider web of contemplation –
but an autobiography can only survive in ashes,
persistence is extinction.
It is certainly a sign: whoever has seen it,
will always return to you.

Each knows his own: his pride
was not an escape, his humility
was not a meanness, his obscure
earth-bound flash
was not the fizzle of a wet match.

1961

BEN BELITT

Little Testament

This thing that darkles and dazzles at night
in the husk of my head –
snailtrack in mother-of-pearl,
smashed emery glass – it could never
light up a church or a work-table
or be trimmed like a lamp by the black and the red
of the clerical.
Eye's apple, iris: it is all
I can give as my warranty:
Faith's keepsake, an embattled presumption that burned
like a hard log on a hearth, at long length.
Look well to the ashes, in that mirror
when all the lamps gutter
and the pace of the dancer is timed to a hellish
sardana, and Lucifer, Prince of Darkness, is seen
on a bowsprit on the Thames or the Seine or the Hudson,
beating bituminous wings, half
shorn from his shoulders with the strain of it. "Time's up!"
he will tell you. This thing that I leave is no charm
against hurricane
hung on a cobweb of memory:
but histories end and begin in a cinder
and only extinction is viable.
The sign was a lucky one: whoever has seen it
cannot fail to retrieve you.
Like calls to like: our pride was no trick
of escape, nor our meekness

ignoble, and the tenuous glimmer
that we grated down there was not struck by the stick of
    a match.

1962

CID CORMAN (1924–2004)

Corman was originally a Bostonian, educated at the Boston Latin School and Tufts University. He taught in Italy for ten years before settling in Japan. He was the creator and the virtuoso editor of *Origin*. The best known of his more than one hundred books is probably *Sun Rock Man* (1962), unless it is *Livingdying* (1970). He published translations of René Char (*Leaves of Hypnos*, 1973) and Basho (*Back Roads to Far Towns*, 1996).

The Prisoner's Dream

Daybreak and night hardly vary here.

Zigzagging flocks over the breastworks
on days of battle, my only wings,
an edge of polar air,
the warden's eye at the peephole,
crack of nuts crushed, an oily
hiss from the pits, barbecues
real or supposed – but the straw is gold,
the wine-lit lantern a hearth
when I sleep and think myself at your feet.

The purge always hard, unreasonable.
They say that he who recants and signs
may be saved from this massacre of geese;
that he who groans and complains
and confesses and denounces, grabs for the scummer
rather than end up in the pâté
destined for the pestilential Gods.

Slow-witted, body sore
from the prickly litter I am fused
to the flight of the moth grinding
my sole to dust on the paved floor,
to the iridescent kimonos of lights
aired at dawn from the high towers,
I've sniffed in the wind the crispness
of biscuits from the ovens,
have gazed around me, stirred up
rainbows on spidery horizons
and petals on the trelliswork of bars,
have lifted myself up, and fallen back
down there where a century is a minute –

and the blows keep coming and the paces,
and I still don't know if at the banquet I'm to be
the joker or the joke. The waiting is long,
the dream I have of you is not over.

1963

SATURA

1971

GAVIN EWART (1916–95)

Ewart was educated at Christ's College, Cambridge, and served in
the Royal Artillery during the war, some of the time in Italy. A pre-
cocious poet – his first poem, "Phallus in Wonderland," was pub-
lished in Geoffrey Grigson's *New Verses* in 1933 – he became an
abundant one after the age of fifty-five. Besides the poem printed here,
Ewart translated poems by Luciano Erba, Mario Luzi, and Pasolini.
His *Collected Poems* was published in 1991.

Thrust and Riposte

1

"Arsenio" (she writes to me), "I, breathing gently here
between my dismal cypresses, think that
the time has come, now, to suspend the suspension
of every worldly deception –
wished for by you for me;
that it is time to unfurl the sails and suspend
the *epoche*.

Not to mention that it is the black season
and the doves with trembling wings flown South.
Living on memories – I can no longer.
Better the bite of the ice than your sleepwalker's
lethargy, O late awakener!"

2

Scarcely emerged from adolescence,
for half my life I was thrown
into the Augean stables.

I did not find two thousand oxen,
nor did I see any animals – ever –
and yet in the pathways,
thicker and thicker with dung,
walking was difficult,
breathing was difficult –
the human bellowing grew from day to day.

He, the Great One, was never seen.
The mob however waited for him
for the Present Arms. Over-filled funnels
pitchforks and spits, a foul-smelling string
of *saltimbocca*. And yet, you know,
not once did He put forth
fold of cloak or point of crown
above the faecal ebony ramparts!

Then from year to year – who counted the
seasons any more in that thick mist? – a hand
feeling for the tiniest openings
worked in its memorial – a curl
of Gerti's, a caged cricket, the last trace
of Liuba's passing, the microfilm
of a euphuistic sonnet (slipped
from Clizia's fingers as she slept),
a wooden sandal-click (the lame
housemaid of Monghidoro)
                                        until from the crevices
the fanning fire of a machine-gun pushed us back,
tired shovellers caught in the act
by the foreign police-chiefs of the mud.

And at last the fall – beyond belief!

To free us, to call together the intricate
tunnels into a lake – all the work of a moment
for that twisted Alpheus! Who would have
thought it! What did that new mire mean?
and the breathing of other, but similar, stenches?
and the whirlpool-whirling on rafts of dung?
Was that the sun, that filthy grub from a sewer,
over the chimney-pots?
Were they men perhaps,
true living men,
the huge ants on the landing-stages

....
(I think
that perhaps you've stopped reading me.
But now you know all of me,
of my prison and my life afterwards;
now you know that the eagle can't be born
of a mouse).

1980

HARRY THOMAS

Xenia I

1

Dear little insect
whom we called Mosca – I don't know why –,
this evening just before dark
while I was reading Deutero-Isaiah
you reappeared at my side,
but not having your glasses
you couldn't see me,
and without their glinting
I couldn't be sure
it was you in the dusk.

2

Without glasses or antennae,
a poor insect who had wings
only in imagination,
a Bible coming unbound
and largely unreliable,
the black of night, a lightning flash,
a thunderclap, and then
no storm. Can it be
you were gone so quickly
without saying a word?
But it's ridiculous to think
you still had lips.

3

At the Saint James in Paris I'll have to ask
for a single room (they don't like
the odd guest). And also at your faux
Byzantium hotel in Venice;
and then immediately go down to find
the switchboard operators' cubbyhole,
those girls who were always your friends;
only to give up again,
the telephone connection lost,
the desire of having you back,
if only in one habit or gesture.

4

For the afterlife we had devised
a whistle, a sign of recognition.
I'm trying variations of it in the hope
We're all already dead without knowing it.

5

I've never understood
whether I was your dog,
faithful and sick with distemper,
or you were mine.
To others you were a myopic insect
at a loss in the blah-blah
of high society. They were naive,
those clever ones. They didn't know
they were your laughingstock:
that even in the dark you made them out
unmasking them

with that infallible sense of yours,
your bat-radar.

6

It never crossed your mind to write prose or verse
and so leave behind you traces of yourself.
That was your charm and then my self-disgust.
It was also my fear –
that you'd drive me back
into the croaking mire
of the neoteroi.

7

The self-pity, endless pain and anguish
of one who worships this world and hopes without hope
for another ... (Who dares to speak of another world?).
....
"Strange piety..." (Azucena, Act II).

8

Your speech, so sparing and unguarded,
remains the one thing that satisfies me.
But the accent is different, the color changed.
I'll get accustomed to hearing you or deciphering you
in the ticking of the teletype,
in the shifting smoke
        of my Brissago cigars.

9

Listening was the only way you had of seeing.
Now the phone bill is down to next to nothing.

10

"Did she pray?" "Yes, she prayed to St. Anthony
because he helps to find
lost umbrellas and other things
from St. Hermes' closet."
"Only for that?" "Also for her dead
and for me."
                    "That's enough," said the priest.

11

To remember your tears (mine numbered twice as many)
isn't to blot out your bursts of laughter.
They were like a deposit on your private
Last Judgment, which unfortunately never came to pass.

12

Spring comes along at a mole's pace.
I won't hear you any more talking of poisonous
antibiotics, the spike in your femur,
the patrimony you were fleeced of
by a predatory nonentity.

Spring approaches with its thick fogs,
longer days, and unbearable hours.
I won't hear you any more struggling
with time, ghosts, or the logistical
problems of summer.

13

Your brother died young; you were
the dishevelled girl who looks out at me

"posed" in an oval portrait.
He wrote music, unpublished, unheard,
now buried in a trunk or rotted away.
Perhaps someone's reinventing it
unwittingly, if what's written is written.
I loved him without having known him.
Except for you, no one remembered him.
I made no inquiries; now there's no point.
After you I'm the only one left
for whom he ever existed. But it's possible,
you know, to love a shade,
being shades ourselves.

14

They say that mine
is a poetry of not belonging.
But if it was yours it was someone's –
you who are no longer form, but essence.
They say that the highest poetry
praises the Oneness of life as it flees,
denying that the tortoise
is quicker than lightning.
Only you knew that motion
is not different from stasis,
that the void is fullness and a clear sky
the most diffuse of clouds.
So I understand better your long journey
imprisoned in bandages and plasters.
And yet it doesn't comfort me
to know that as one or as two
we are a single thing.

HARRY THOMAS

Xenia II

1

Death didn't concern you.
Though among the dead were your two dogs
and the asylum doctor known as the Demented Uncle,
as well as your mother with her "speciality"
of rice and frogs – a Milanese triumph –,
and even your father, who evening and morning
watches me from a miniature
portrait on the wall.
Despite all this, death didn't concern you.

It was I who went to the funerals,
unseen in a taxi standing a ways off
to avoid tears and irritations. Not even
life and its exhibitions of vanity and greed
mattered to you, and so
so much less the universal gangrenes
that transform men into wolves.

A tabula rasa; except
that there came a point, incomprehensible to me,
and this point *concerned you*.

2

You were often reminded (I seldom was) of Herr Cap.
"I saw him on Ischia, on the bus, maybe twice.
He's a lawyer from Klagenfurt, the one who sends his best
    wishes.

He was supposed to come for a visit."

And finally he comes. I tell him everything; he's dumb-
    founded.
It seems it's a catastrophe for him as well. For a while he
    says nothing.
Then he stands up, mumbling and stiff, bows, and assures
    me
he'll send his best wishes.
                              It's strange
how the most unlikely people turned out to understand you.
Counsellor Cap. What a name! And Celia. What became of
    her?

3

For a long time the shoehorn was missing,
that rusted tin horn we took with us everywhere,
though to carry so indecorous a thing
among the tombac and stucco seemed indecent.
It must have been at the Danieli that I forgot
to put it back into the suitcase or small bag.
I'm sure that Hedia the chambermaid threw it
into the Grand Canal. And how could I have written
that I was searching for three inches of tin?
Prestige (*ours*) had to be saved
and Hedia, the faithful, had done it.

4

Uncannily
escaping from the jaws of Etna
or the teeth of ice,
you came out
with incredible revelations.

Mangano, the good surgeon, witnessed one:
you exposed him as the Black Shirts' cudgel,
and he smiled.
That was you: even on the edge of the abyss
sweetness and terror in a single note.

5

I've descended, your arm in mine, almost a million stairs
and now that you're not here a void opens at every step.
Even so, our long journey was brief.
Mine still goes on, though I no longer feel the need
for connections, reservations,
mix-ups, the scorn of those who believe
that reality is what one sees.

I've descended millions of stairs, your arm in mine,
not, of course, because four eyes see better than two.
I descended them with you because I knew
that between us the only true pupils,
however clouded over, were yours.

6

The wine steward poured you a little
Inferno. And you, frightened: "Must I drink it?
Isn't it enough to be there slowly burning?"

7

"I've never been sure of being in the world."
"How clever," you responded, "and me?"
"Oh, you've nibbled at the world's edges,
if only in homeopathic doses. But I..."

8

"And Paradise? Does paradise exist?"
"I believe so, Signora,
but no one drinks sweet wines anymore."

9

Nuns and widows, those deadly,
malodorous, professional mourners,
you wouldn't let yourself look at them.
You were sure that even he
who has a thousand eyes
turns away from them.
The all-seeing, him ... judicious,
you didn't call him god,
not even with a small g.

10

I'd been looking a long time
when finally I found you in a bar
on the Avenida de Liberdada. You didn't know
a single word of Portuguese – or rather,
knew a single word: Madeira. And a small glass came
along with a plate of shrimp.

That evening they likened me to illustrious
Lusitanians with unpronounceable names
and, in addition, to Carducci.
I saw you, unimpressed, hidden in a crowd,
laughing so hard you were crying;
bored, perhaps, but with compunction.

11

Resurfacing out of an infinity of time,
Celia the Phillipina called
just to see how you were doing.
"I believe she's well," I said,
"maybe better than before." "What? You believe?
Isn't she there?" "Maybe more than before, but…
Celia, try to understand…"

On the other end of the line,

in Manila or some other
name on the atlas, stammering
stymied even her. And she slammed down the phone.

12

The hawks
always too far away for you,
you rarely saw them really well.
The one at Etretat that watched
the clumsy flights of its young.
Two others in Greece, on the road to Delphi,
a scuffle of soft feathers, two beaks,
young, ardent and harmless.

You liked life ripped to shreds,
whatever broke free of its unbearable
form.

13

I have hung up in my room the daguerreotype
of your father as a child: it's more than a century old.
In the absence of my own (a confused thing),
I try to reconstruct, unsuccessfully, your pedigree.

We aren't horses, our ancestors' lines
aren't in the books. Those who presumed
to know such things did not themselves exist,
nor did we for them. And so? It's still the case
that something happened, perhaps a nothing
that is everything.

14

The flood has covered the clutter of furniture,
papers, and paintings that filled
a basement locked with a double lock.
Perhaps the moroccan-bound books fought blindly,
and so too the endless dedications of Du Bos,
the wax seal with Ezra's beard,
Alain's Valery, the first edition
of *Canti orfici* – not to mention some shaving
brushes, a thousand trifles and all
your brother Silvio's music.
Ten, twelve days in the atrocious hold
of naphta and dung. Surely they suffered
a lot before losing their identity.
I too am encrusted up to the neck,
but my civil status was dubious from the start.
It's not muck that besieges me, but the events
of a reality that's unbelievable
and never believed in.
In the face of it all, courage
was the first gift you gave me,
and perhaps you didn't know it.

G. SINGH

Late in the Night

One can't converse with shades
on the phone.
During our mute dialogues there is
no microphone boom or loudspeaker.
However, even words serve
when they don't concern us, picked up
by mistake by a telephone operator
and relayed to someone who
isn't there, doesn't hear.
Once they came from Vancouver
late in the night while I was waiting
for a call from Milan.
At first I was taken aback,
but then hoped that the mix-up would continue.
One voice from the Pacific, the other
from the lagoon. At that time
the two voices talked freely as never
before. Then nothing happened,
we assured the operator that
everything was perfect, in order,
and could continue, in fact *must* continue.
Nor did we ever know who'd foot the bill
for that miracle.
But I didn't remember a single word.
The time zone was different, the other
voice wasn't there, and I
wasn't there for her, even the languages
got mixed up, a hotchpotch of jargons,

curses and laughter. By now
after all these years
the other voice has forgotten and perhaps
thinks I'm dead. I think
it's she who is dead, but was
alive for a second at least,
and did not know it.

1976

JEREMY REED

Backward Glance

You turn around and it's another century.
You've changed, the dusted sandpaper's
rubbed each prominent line thinner,
yet words were written on the page of life
and still, magnified by the light define
a hieroglyphic sign, its blaze clearer
than any diadem which blinded you...
The moment won't recur: your tiny form
emerging from a lit hovercraft hatch
or come up from skindiving trailing weed
from the ripcurrent's evidence of how
dimensions interact. Perhaps in time
you'll ascend escalators to temples
and walk as one living with the masked dead,
unsure if the procession's illusion,
choice or a dictate your psyche answered.
And how determine who is the bull's eye
marked out for the inexorable arrow?
Knowledge is given in a bright instant;
we open the segments of the orange,
and realise that walking in this life
we never know if we're alive or dead.
Nothing's stable. The word dries on the change...

1990

LAWRENCE KART (b. 1942)

Kart was for many years the literary editor of the *Chicago Tribune*.
His translation of Montale's *Mottetti* appeared in 1974.

After a Flight

1

There was a thicket of birches trying
to hide the sanatorium where a sufferer
from too much love of life was balanced
between all and nothingness, bored.
A chirping cricket, the perfect
complement to the clinic's design,
echoed the cuckoo you'd heard before
in Indonesia at a lesser price.
There were birch trees, a Swiss nurse,
three or four idiots in the courtyard,
on the bedstand an album of exotic birds,
the telephone and a few chocolates.
And, of course, I was there too, another
old nuisance attempting to give you
a comfort you could have lavished on us
if only we'd had the eyes to see it. I did.

2

You don't have that sacerdotal walk
one learns abroad from Jacques-Dalcroze,
more like mincing than a ritual.
Yours came from Oceania, in your heel
the bones of a fish. Relations, doctors
and interns swirl about you, unaware

that your coral reefs are not Le Focette
but the spume of beyond, an exit
from life on this earth. Those three
fishbones in your foot, not sharkfins
one could eat. And then they bundle you
in artificial sleep. Long-distance dialing,
grumbles from go-betweens, and you murmur
a little on the telephone. The line yields
nothing else, not even the sound of feet
on a carpet. The aquarium sleeps.

3

If a whirlwind had snapped you up
setting you down in the celestial world
of Amerindians, who more and more to elude
the white man enmesh themselves in their
vegetal web, you would have been greeted
by garlands of drums, though your eyes
are not long and narrow like a Mongol's.
Surely their flight has gone on
for generations. Yours, a brief one,
at least has saved you from the darkness
or claw that held you hostage. And now
one doesn't need a telephone to reach you.

4

My road has passed among
indistinguishable demons and gods.
It was all a bazaar of beards and masks,
a pungent chatter in Volapük and Guarani
no one could understand. Don't ask now
why I settled on you, with what face
and what sound you entered this head

deafened by too much traffic noise.
At last for me some knot or link was
completed, which you evidently knew
nothing about. The first time we met
you wandered away, your mind vague
as smoke, and threw from the window
a glass, a shoe, and almost yourself,
if I hadn't been there. And yet you
still know nothing about it: dream,
noose or snare, it's useless to ask.
Surely your road, too,
was straddling hell, as if to say
farewell to an uninhabitable elysium.

5

While I think of you the leaves turn
on the calendar. A cruel time of year
and time itself even deadlier. What was
best in you burst out amid resinous trees,
briar patches, river banks, the croaking
of frogs, and brief flights of stilt birds
with names I didn't know (we pretended
they were Knights of Italy!) as I slept
wide awake amid my musty books and notes.
And I burst out, too, with the worst in me:
the wish to reascend the years, to outwit
Cronos with a thousand ruses. It is said
I believe in nothing but miracles. You
believe in yourself, perhaps, or let others
choose to make what they will of you. Which
is more than human, the privilege of those
who without knowing it hold up the world.

6

When we came to the village of the Nazi
massacre, Sant' Anna, beneath a sheer peak
of rock, I watched you scramble doe-like
to the top with a Polish exile and your
water-rat guide, best goat of all.
At the monument in the square I stood
five hours counting the dead, foolishly
imagining, *honoris causa*, that my name
was there. At nightfall a jolting
motorboat took us down Burlamacca,
canal of filth into which an ersatz
oil plant exudes boiling water,
perhaps as a preview of hell.
Burlamacchi, Caponsacchi ... shades
of heresies, of unreadable poems.
Poetry and sewers (though I didn't
say it) are two, inseparable themes.

7

Slow to accept neologisms, I was
doubtful at first, half-awake, whether
Hovercraft or Hydrofoil was the winged
creature on which I planned to steal you
furtively away. Meanwhile you had fled
with a lucky water rat, who was quicker
than I and alas much younger. Wandering
slowly the whole long day, I reflected
no such thoughts had passed between Lear
and Cordelia, and my comparison collapsed.
With a group I toured the Etruscan
tombs, lairs of aristocrats with the look
of thieves, and old Livorno's prison-like

Piranesian streets. Coming back I tunneled
through a heap of rubbish and was astounded
by the sky, almost terrified at its return.
The tragic parallel had vanished like smoke
since, above all, I'm not even your father.

8

I cannot breathe without you. Keats
to Fanny Brawne, spared by him from
obscurity. Strange that my case, permit me,
should be different. I breathe much better
with you far away. Proximity brings
past events back to me: not what occurred
but what we thought would happen, like
vinegar or smelling salts one puts aside
for future use (though these days broken
hearts are such trifles that no one swoons).
The facts alone remain to take the blow,
a structure that collapses with a corpse
in plain view. To speak of it, I won't even
try, but this I know: if you read me you feel
the necessary impulse was furnished by you
and the rest matters little (provided *I*
not be silent).

1975

EAMON GRENNAN

Venetian Piece

Just following orders, the talkative doorman –
grinning like one of Dante's devils –
said it was forbidden to disturb
the man of bullfights and safaris.
I beg him to try, I'm a friend of Pound's
(I exaggerated a little) and so deserve
some special treatment. Who knows...
He picks up the receiver, talks, listens,
gabbles some more and – who'd believe it! –
Hemingway the bear has swallowed the hook.
He's still in bed. Only his eyes appear
and his spots of eczema, peering out
from underneath the fur blanket. Two
or three empty bottles of Merlot –
outriders of the great troop to follow.
Down in the restaurant everyone's eating.
We don't talk about him but our dear friend
Adrienne Monnier, Rue de l'Odeon,
Sylvia Beach, Larbaud, the roaring 'twenties,
the braying 'fifties. Paris a pigsty, ditto London,
New York *stinking*, plague-ridden. Nothing
to hunt in the marshes. No wild duck, no girls,
not even the idea for another book *like that*.
We draw up a list of common friends
whose names I pay no heed to. Everything
is *rotten*, rotten. Almost in tears,
he insists I send him no more visitors

like myself – all the worse if intelligent. Then
he gets up, bundles himself in his bathrobe,
and bids me *adieu* at the door with a hug. He lived
two years after that and, dying twice,
had time to read his own obituaries.

WILLIAM ARROWSMITH

Rebecca

Every day I find myself coming up short:
I'm missing the total.
The items to be added are perfectly right,
but the overall total?
Rebecca watered her camels
and herself too.
I attend to pen and messkit
for myself and for others.
Rebecca was thirsty, I'm starved,
but we won't be absolved.
There wasn't much water in the wadi, a few puddles maybe,
and not much kindling in my kitchen either.
Still, for ourselves, for everyone, we tried, in smoke,
in mud, with a few live bipeds or even quadrupeds.
O meek Rebecca whom I never met!
Hardly a handful of centuries divides us,
the twinkling of an eye for those who grasp your teaching.
Only the divine is total in sip and crumb.
Only death triumphs when you ask for both.

1998

W. S. DI PIERO

Lights and Colors

You always appear dressed in that red bed-jacket,
your eyes puffed by sleep. What have they seen?
I have no way to explain these silent visitations.
It's probably just light glancing off your glasses,
a kind of mirror flash slicing the darkness.
Last time it happened, I saw a homely,
apricot-colored worm dragging itself
across the throw rug. It wasn't easy to scoop it
with a slip of paper and toss it down, still alive,
into the courtyard. It weighed no more than you.

DIARIO DEL '71 E DEL '72
Diary of '71 and '72
1973

G. SINGH

The Carillon Pendulum Clock

The old pendulum clock with the carillon
came from France perhaps
at the time of the Second Empire.
So faint was its voice that it neither
trilled nor pealed but exhaled
instead of sounding, the entrance
of Escamillo or the bells of Corneville
which were its novelty when someone bought it,
perhaps the great-grandfather who ended up
in a lunatic asylum and was buried
without regrets, obituary or other
such notices which might have embarrassed
his unborn grandchildren. They came later
and lived without remembering him
who carried that object within
inhospitable walls lashed by
the furies of the southwest gales
– and which of them heard its alarm?
It was a call that of course woke no one who wasn't
already awake. Only I, being always sleepless,
heard one dawn the vocal ectoplasm,
the echo of the *toriada*, but just for a second.
Then the voice from the case didn't die out
but spoke almost inaudibly and said
there isn't a spring nor electric charge
that won't run down one day.
I who was Time, abandon it,
and say to you, my only listener,
try to live outside of time,

which no one can measure. Then the voice
was silent and the clock remained
hung on the wall for years.
Probably one can still trace its outline
on the plaster.

1976

HARRY THOMAS

Sorapis, 40 Years Ago

I've never liked the mountains much,
and I detest the Alps. I've never seen
the Andes or the Cordilleras.
Only the Sierra de Guadarrama enraptured me,
gentle in its ascent and with fallow deer
on the peaks – stags,
according to the tourist brochure.
Only the electric air of the Engadine
took our breath away, my little insect,
but it wasn't so rich that it made us say
hic manebimus.
Among the lakes only that of Sorapis
was a great discovery. It had the solitude
of marmots more heard of than glimpsed
and the air of Celestials. But what a road
for getting there! The first time
I took it alone in order to see
if your eyes could penetrate the clouds
zigzagging among the high slabs of ice.
And how long it was! and made easy only
in the first stretch, a dark stand of conifers,
by the ringing alarm of jays.
Then holding you by the hand, I guided you
up to the top, an empty hut.
That was our lake: a few spans of water,
two lives much too young to be old
and much too old to feel we were young.
We discovered then what age is.

It has nothing to do with time,
but is something that says, that makes us say,
we are here, a miracle
that cannot repeat itself. By comparison
youth is the vilest of deceptions.

2000

QUADERNO DEL
QUATTRO ANNI
Notebook of Four Years

1977

JORIE GRAHAM (b. 1951) and
DANIEL HALPERN (b. 1945)

As a child Graham lived for some time in Italy. She is the author
of several books of poetry, including *The Dream of the Unified
Field: Poems 1974–1994* (1995) and *Swarm* (1999). She teaches at
Harvard.

Halpern founded *Antaeus* and the Ecco Press. Among his many
books are *Selected Poems* (1994), *Something Shining* (1999), and
Halpern's Guide to the Essential Restaurants of Italy (1990). He
teaches at Columbia.

I lived on the third floor in those days
and from one end of a row of hedges
Galiffa, the little dog, could see me –
with great leaps off the winding staircase
he would come over to me. Now I can't remember
if he died in our house, if he was buried,
and if so, when and where. All I remember
is that leap and his bark,
just as little more remains of great loves
when they're not of despair and death.
But this wasn't the case with that little dog
with the long ears, who had a name
invented by the farmer's son
who was my age, illiterate and strangely
less alive than the dog that lives in my sleeplessness.

1976

JORIE GRAHAM and
DANIEL HALPERN

The Day of the Dead

Gina has lit a candle for her dead.
She's lit it in the kitchen –
the dead are many, and they are far away.
We must think back to when she was a child
and her breakfast was a handful of dried chestnuts.
We must call forth a small and old father,
his ways of finding a drop or two of sweet wine.
Because there was only enough money to feed the pigs
she took to the fields,
there was no money for his wine,
his candy and nuts.
Among the dead we put the teacher
whose whip cut her frozen fingers as a child.
Dead too is someone who lives – some half-living –
down near the ferry. It's a crowd
and yet it's nothing –
she never took the pigs to the fields.

1976

ANTHONY BURGESS (1917–93)

Born in Manchester, Burgess was descended on both sides from Catholics "obstinate in their adherence to Rome." At the age of eleven, he won a scholarship to Xaverian College, but was an apostate by the time he entered Manchester University in 1937. He spent the war years as a pianist and arranger in the Royal Army Medical Corps and then the Army Education Corps. He was a talented composer as well as a great novelist. From 1970 to 1975 he and his second wife, Liana Macellari, an Italian translator of English fiction, lived in Rome. Burgess's novels set in Italy are *MF* (1971), *Beard's Roman Women* (1976), and *ABBA ABBA* (1977), this last a novel of Keats's final days that imagines him in the company of Belli, the great Italian dialect poet. Burgess's translation of a number of Belli's sonnets appear as an appendix to the novel. He also published a translation of the libretto of *Carmen* (1986). He contributed the following translation to a special Alberti issue of *The Malahat Review*. Montale entitled the poem "L'eroismo" ("Heroism"). What may look like confusion in Burgess's title is really adulating wit, for in the poem Montale did write called "Per un Omaggio a Rimbaud" (see Jeremy Reed's translation above), he regards Rimbaud as a poet in exile, like Alberti.

For Un Omaggio a Rafael Alberti

Clitia (sunflower nymph of Apollo)
Put it often in my head that I should join the
Spanish fighters. More than once I have seen myself
Dead at Guadalajara or else, a survivor, a famous
Veteran awkward on his feet after years in the galley.
But none of this happened – not even the
Word flood of the official orator bayed in glory,
Nor the plod of lofty duty gifted my fate.

But where could I have fought – I, no lover of the
Droves of the empty and the dispossessed?
Still, I remember one thing: a prisoner I took
Who had a Rilke in his pocket, he and I friends
For a minute or two. Pointless then the
Fatigue, bomb thud, wearing tacktack of the snipers.
Pointless to her too, who lacked love of
Fatherlands, possessed one only by chance.

1978

ALTRI VERSI
E POESIE DISPERSE

Other Verses and Uncollected Poems

1981

JONATHAN GALASSI

Winter lingers on. The sun is doled out
with a dropper. Isn't it strange that we,
lords and perhaps inventors of the universe,
to understand a piece of it, must trust
the charlatans and soothsayers mushrooming everywhere?
It seems obvious the Gods
are beginning to tire of their presumptive
children or wards.
Even clearer that, Gods or demigods,
they in turn have quit
their employers, if they ever had any.
But...

1984

JAMIE McKENDRICK

The Earth's Rind

The Earth's rind is finer, more close-grained
than an apple's skin – if we assume
the material world is not
just an illusion. Nonetheless
we're stuck in this nothing, if such
we admit it is, up to our necks.
The pessimists say that what sticks
us here is everything we've made
to replace the gods. But the old God's
still faithful followers assert
this substitution didn't take.
Perhaps He'll come, they say, in person
to prize us from the magma limb
by limb. So we live and are
a double life, even if the self-
adoring would choose only one.
O mother Earth, O Heaven
of celestial beings – it's this
that's the problem,
that makes us mad and shriller than
a bird in lime.

1993

JONATHAN GALASSI

To My Friend Pea

When Leopoldo Fregoli heard the footfall of death
he put on his tails, set a flower in his lapel
and ordered the waiter, Serve lunch.
Pea told me this about the end of a man he greatly admired.
Another time he talked about a winter in Sarzana
and all the ice of that exile
with a stoic indifference that masked his compassion.
Compassion for everything: for men, and a bit less for
        himself.
I knew him for thirty years or more as an impresario,
a shaper of words and men.
Today it seems everyone's forgotten him
and somehow the news has reached him too
without upsetting him. He's taking notes
to tell us what's beyond the clouds,
beyond the blue, beyond the junkheap of the world
we were tossed on by good grace.
Just a few lines in a notebook no publisher
will ever be able to print; perhaps it will be read
at a congress of demons and gods
the date of which is unknown since it isn't in time.

1984

N. S. THOMPSON (b. 1950)

Thompson was curator at the Casa Guidi, once the home of the Brownings in Florence. He is now at Christ Church, Oxford. He has translated three books of Italian prose, including *The Crux* (1990), a political crime novel by Giampaolo Rugarli.

Nixon in Rome

In limited numbers, scrutinised
but also exposed to the showers of stones and insults,
we're invited to the banquet
for the welcome Guest. Black tie, no
tails or decorations. It's no use brushing
sashes and useless stuff. We'll be the chosen few
under the flashbulbs, mentioned in the afternoon
newspapers that no one reads.
We'll have the Cuirassiers, a Cardinal,
former Excellencies and the highest guarantors
of the Constitution,
Sherry consommé, salmon, asparagus
eaten with tongs, Roederer *brut*,
speeches, interpreters, the orchestra
that will play "Rhapsody in Blue"
and Jommelli and Boccherini to close.
The chef has been engaged in a competition
and only for him, perhaps, are we at the Epiphany
of a New Way.
The Guest has arrived; some
deny that he may have been substituted.
The guests don't seem the same.

Perhaps the banquet will be postponed. But
we rise to our feet for the toasts with our glasses and
look each other in the face. Providing Offenbach's
Brigands have not sat down in our places
everything seems normal. The director
of the special services says so.

1981

DAVID KELLER (b. 1941) and
DONALD SHEEHAN (b. 1940)

Keller and Sheehan translated the five poems in their *Satura* (1969)
while students in Walter Hamady's typography class at the Univer-
sity of Wisconsin. Keller now lives in New Jersey. *Trouble in His-
tory* (2000) is his most recent book of poems. Sheehan is a Senior
Lecturer at Dartmouth College and Director of the Frost Place in
Franconia, New Hampshire.

Afloat

Clearest mornings,
when the azure's an illusion that does not deceive,
growing immense with life,
a flood stream that has no banks or inlet
and goes for ever,
and stays – infinitely.

Then the rising street sounds and calls
are the crack in the window
or the stone that falls
in the lake's mirror to wrinkle it.

And the children's shouts
and the liquid cheeping of sparrows
darting between the eaves
are latticeworks golden
over a live, cobalt surface,
momentary...

Wait, it's lost in the net of echoes,
in the cloud of frost
descending over the thinned-out trees
and from it there follows a murmur
of the restless sea,
you half-wish, and yet fear
the remote heart would cease,
beat no more! But each time you invite it,
the pulses come more strongly like
a clock unnoticed in the room
of a hotel from the first movement at dawn.

Listen then,
even if they repeat only that you may
stop mid-way, or beyond the sea view,
that there's no rest for us,
but farther, still farther turning,
and that the journey is always to begin anew.

1969

DAVID KELLER and
DONALD SHEEHAN

In a Void

The sun's crest had gotten itself twisted
among the garden trellises, and on the shore
a sluggish rowboat seemed half-asleep.
No sound had come from the day
under the clear arch,
nor the skip
of a pine cone or bud snapping
outside the walls.

The silence had swallowed everything,
our boat hadn't come to a standstill,
it drew a mark on the sand, a sign so long
suspended high up had dropped.

Now the ground was a rim overflowing,
weight loose in the dazzle,
the flame was the foam on the darkness,
the ditch grew larger, much too deep
for the anchor and for us
                              until suddenly
something happened around us, the rampart closed
in its halves, nothing and everything was lost,
and I awoke at the sound of your lips,
mute before – and since then held prisoner
both of us in the vein that in crystal,
invisibly, waits for its day.

1969

HOMAGES TO MONTALE

CHARLES WRIGHT

This poem from Wright's *Bloodlines* (1975) is the last in a series of twenty poems entitled "Tattoos." The third stanza is an adaptation of the end of Montale's "Serenata indiana" (see George Kay's translation on page 127).

You stand in your shoes, two shiny graves
Dogging your footsteps;
You spread your fingers, ten stalks
Enclosing your right of way;
You yip with pain in your little mouth.

And this is where the ash falls.
And this is the time it took to get here –
And yours, too, is the stall, the wet wings
Arriving, and the beak.
And yours the thump, and the soft voice:

The octopus on the reef's edge, who slides
His fat fingers among the cracks,
Can use you. You've prayed to him,
In fact, and don't know it.
You *are* him, and think yourself yourself.

1973

JONATHAN GALASSI

Montale's Grave

Now that the ticket to eternity
has your name on it, we are here to pay
the awkward tribute post-modernity
allows to those who think they think your way

but hear you only faintly, filtered through
a gauze of echoes, sounding in a voice
that could be counterfeit; and yet the noise
seems to expand our notion of the true.

An ivory forehead, landscape drunk on light,
mother-of-pearl that flashes in the night:
intimations of the miracle
when the null steps forward as the all –

these were signals, sparks that spattered from
the anvil of illusions where you learned
the music of a generation burned
by an old myth: the end that will not come.

There is no other myth. This sun-drenched yard
proves it, freighted with the waiting dead,
where votive plastic hyacinths relay
the promise of one more technicolor day

– the promise that is vouchsafed to you, scribe,
and your dictator, while your names get blurred
with all the others, like your hardest word
dissolving in the language of the tribe.

1988

RACHEL WETZSTEON

Blind Date

Siren I have never seen,
only begetter of a brain where
synapses howl from crag to
crag, vast eons of daytime stretching
between them, popper of
flavorless gum, vision
in flames and taffeta, merry
wisecracker, dream in white and
would-be harpy, when you sprang,
gung-ho and tiara-first, out
of the mouth of the god who praised you,
was it you who committed atrocities
of hairspray then and there, or
are you only a slave
of the void who sees you
plucking at damaged harps, pecking
at heartstrings? When you two tango
down the runway, where will you put
your pitchfork? Is it good
to be young? When you simper
under balloons (black for appearances,
red for later, corruption's favorite
colors), what radiant halo
favors you, flees from me? What night
of no moon beckons? What
does he have in store for you? Reporter
to no one, aspiring tart and
unwilling virgin, can't you

pack up all your tricks and
bother another?

1994

GEOFFREY HILL (b. 1932)

Hill was educated at Oxford and taught for many years at Leeds University and later at Cambridge University. Since 1987 he has been a professor at Boston University. He is the author of several books of poetry, including *New and Collected Poems 1952–1992* (1994) and *The Triumph of Love* (1998), from which the following section is excerpted.

CXXXIV

It surprises me not at all that your
private, marginal, uncommitted writing –
this is to be in code – came at the end
to the forum of world acclaim. *Decenza* –
your term – I leave unchallenged; decorum
aloof from conformity; not a mask
of power's harsh suavities. [Internal
evidence identifies the late
Eugenio Montale as the undoubted
subject of this address – ED.] It sets you
high among the virtuous *avvocati* –
the judges with a grasp of such vocation –
and puts you with the place-brokers, purveyors
of counsel, publishers, editors,
and senators-for-life; a civic conscience
attested by comedy: twenty-five years
with the *Nuove Corriere della Sera*
as leader-writer and critic of first nights;
still your own man; publicities, public life,
the ante room to the presence-chamber
of self-containment. (Machiavelli described
entering his study, robed as if for Court.)

But one man's privacy is another's
crowded *at home* – we are that circumscribed.
Machado who, to say the least, is your
grand equal, sat out his solitude, habitué
of small, shaky, wicker or zinc tables –
still-life with bottle, glass, scrawled school-*cahiers* –
put his own voice to slow-drawn induration.
I admire you and have trained my ear
to your muted discords. This rage twists
me, for no reason other than the sight
of anarchy coming to irregular order
with laurels; now with wreaths: Duomo drone-
bell, parade-mask shout, beautifully-caught
scatter of pigeons in brusque upward tumble,
wingbeats held by a blink.

1998

MICHAEL HOFMANN (b. 1957)

Hofmann, the most important English poet of his generation, was born in Freiburg, Germany, and came to England in 1961. He has translated more than two dozen books from the German. His most recent book of poems is *Approximately Nowhere* (1999).

Megrim

Corners of the linden yellow like grapes...
back in July leaves blew. Rain wounds the window,
preoccupies the drainpipes, nourishes –
after a seemly interval – the mould spots
in the cornices. Stray nooses of wisteria
toss purposely, aimlessly, who can say.

1999

ACKNOWLEDGMENTS

For permission to reproduce copyright material in this book, the editor and publisher gratefully acknowledge the following:

WILLIAM ARROWSMITH. "Rebecca," from *Satura 1962–1970* by Eugenio Montale, edited by Rosanna Warren, translated by William Arrowsmith, copyright © 1971 by Arnoldo Mondadori Editore SpA. English text copyright © 1998 by the William Arrowsmith Estate and Rosanna Warren. Copyright © 1992 W.W. Norton & Company, Inc.

SAMUEL BECKETT. "Delta" appeared in *This Quarter* (April, May, June 1930). Reproduced by permission of the Samuel Beckett Estate and Calder Publications Ltd. Special gratitude is owed to Georges Borchardt for arranging the permission for this edition. Translation copyright © 1930 the Estate of Samuel Beckett.

BEN BELITT. "The Balcony," "Lindau," and "Little Testament" are reprinted by the kind permission of the author. Translation copyright © 1962 Ben Belitt.

ROBERT BLY. "On a Letter Not Written" is reprinted by the kind permission of the author. Translation copyright © 1962 Robert Bly.

DANIEL BOSCH. "Falsetto" is reprinted by the kind permission of the author. Translation copyright © 2002 Daniel Bosch.

KEITH BOSLEY. "The Shadow of the Magnolia" is reprinted by the kind permission of the author. Translation copyright © 1972 Keith Bosley.

ANTHONY BURGESS. "For Un Omaggio a Rafael Alberti" is reprinted here by the kind permission of Artellus Press, Ltd. and the Estate of Anthony Burgess. Translation copyright © 1978 the Estate of Anthony Burgess.

JOSEPH CARY. "Don't ask of us the word that squares on every side" is reprinted by the kind permission of the author. Translation copyright © 1968 and 2002 Joseph Cary.

NED CONDINI. "North Wind" is reprinted by the kind permission of the author. Translation copyright © 1987 Ned Condini.

CID CORMAN. "The Prisoner's Dream" was published in *Origin*. Reproduced by kind permission of the author. Translation copyright © 1963 Cid Corman.

ALFRED CORN. "Dora Markus" is reprinted by the kind permission of the author. Translation copyright © 1983 Alfred Corn.

ALFREDO DE PALCHI. "Maybe some morning, walking in dry glass air" is reprinted by the kind permission of Alfredo de Palchi. Translation copyright © 1962 Alfredo de Palchi and the Estate of Sonia Raiziss.

W.S. DI PIERO. "Stanzas" and "Lights and Colors" are reprinted by the kind permission of the author. Translation copyright © 2002 W. S. di Piero.

MAURICE ENGLISH. "Dora Markus." Translation copyright © 1949 the Estate of Maurice English.

GAVIN EWART. "Thrust and Riposte," reprinted with kind permission of Margo Ewart and *Stand*. Translation copyright © 1980 Margo Ewart.

EDITH FARNSWORTH. "Valmorbia, blossoming clouds of plants," "Toward Capua," "The Return," "The Earrings," "Window of Fiesole," "The Ark," "From a Tower" first appeared in *Provisional Conclusions*. Translation copyright © 1970 the Estate of Edith Farnsworth.

DAVID FERRY. "La Farandola dei Fanciulli" first appeared in *Strangers* (1983). It is reprinted here by the kind permission of the author. Translation copyright © 1983 David Ferry. "News from Mount Amiata" is also reprinted here in English by the kind permission of the author. Translation copyright © 1999 David Ferry.

G. S. FRASER. "Bagni Di Lucca," by Eugenio Montale, translation by G. S. Fraser, from *Selected Poems*, copyright © 1965 by New Directions Publishing Corp. Reprinted by permission of New Directions Publishing Corp.

ROBIN FULTON. "Summer" first appeared in *An Italian Quartet: Versions after Saba, Ungaretti, Montale and Quasimodo* (1966). It is reprinted here by the kind permission of the author. Translation copyright © 1966 Robin Fulton.

JONATHAN GALASSI. Farrar, Straus & Giroux, LLC granted their permission to reprint "Eclogue," "From a Swiss Lake," "The House of the Customs Men," "Iris," "On the Threshold," "Punta del Mesco," "Sit the noon out, pale and lost in thought," "Voice That Came with the Coots," "You know: I'm going to lose you," and "Your hand was trying the keyboard," translated by Jonathan Galassi, from *Collected Poems 1920–1954* (1998; rev. 2000) by Eugenio Montale, translated and edited by Jonathan Galassi. Translation copyright © 1998 by Jonathan Galassi.

LEE GERLACH. "The Lemon Trees" is reprinted by kind permission of the author. Translation copyright © 2002 Lee Gerlach.

DANA GIOIA. "Mottetti VI, XV, XVI" by Eugenio Montale, translated from the Italian by Dana Gioia, copyright © 1990 by Dana Gioia. Reprinted from *Mottetti: Poems of Love* with the kind permission of Graywolf Press, Saint Paul, Minnesota.

JORIE GRAHAM. "I lived on the third floor those days" and "The Day of the Dead" are reprinted by the kind permission of the authors. Translation copyright © 1976 Jorie Graham and Daniel Halpern.

EAMON GRENNAN. "*En Route* to Vienna," "To My Mother," "In the Greenhouse," and "Venetian Piece" are reprinted by the kind permission of the author. Translation copyright © 2002 Eamon Grennan.

CHARLES GUENTHER. "Seascape" is reprinted by the kind permission of the author. Translation copyright © 1975 Charles Guenther.

DANIEL HALPERN. "I lived on the third floor those days" and "The Day of the Dead" are reprinted by the kind permission of the authors. Translation copyright © 1976 Jorie Graham and Daniel Halpern.

KEVIN HART. "The Eel" is reprinted by the kind permission of the author. Translation copyright © 1979 Kevin Hart.

GEOFFREY HILL. "CXXXIV," from *The Triumph of Love*, by Geoffrey Hill, copyright © 1998 by Geoffrey Hill. Reprinted by permission of Houghton Mifflin Company. All rights reserved.

MICHAEL HOFMANN. "Megrim," from *Approximately Nowhere* (London: Faber and Faber, 1999). Reprinted by permission of Faber & Faber. Copyright © 1999 Michael Hofmann.

KATE HUGHES. "Do not, o scissors, cut off that face" and "...but so be it. The cornet." Translation copyright © 1980 Kate Hughes.

BEN JOHNSON. "The House of the Customs Men," "New Stanzas," and "The Eel" are reprinted with the permission of the Wylie Agency, Inc. on behalf of the Literary Estate of James Merrill. "The House of the Customs Men," translation copyright © 1952 Ben Johnson and the Literary Estate of James Merrill. "New Stanzas," translation copyright © 1956 Ben Johnson and the Literary Estate of James Merrill. "The Eel," translation copyright © 1953 Ben Johnson and the Literary Estate of James Merrill.

LAWRENCE KART. "After a Flight" is reprinted here by the kind permission of the author. Translation copyright © 1975 Lawrence Kart.

GEORGE KAY. "Flux" and "Indian Serenade" first appeared in *Selected Poems of Eugenio Montale* (1964). Translation copyright © 1964 George Kay.

DAVID KELLER. "Afloat" and "In a Void" first appeared in *Satura: Five Poems by Eugenio Montale* (1969). They are reprinted here by the kind permission of David Keller and Donald Sheehan. Translation copyright © 1969 David Keller and Donald Sheehan.

ROBERT LOWELL. Farrar, Straus & Giroux, LLC granted their permission to reprint "The Coastguard House," "Flux," "Hitlerian Spring," and "Little Testament" by Eugenio Montale and translated by Robert Lowell, from *Collected Poems*, by Robert Lowell. © 2003 by Harriet Lowell and Sheridan Lowell. For "Eastbourne," permission was granted by the Houghton Library, Harvard University. The poem bears the shelf mark *bMS AM 1905 (2780)* in their archives. Translation copyright © 1960 Harriet Lowell and Sheridan Lowell.

J.D. MCCLATCHY. "Rime at the panes; the patients" and "The flower that rehearses" are reprinted here by the kind permission of the author. Translation copyright © 1984 J.D. McClatchy.

JAMIE MCKENDRICK. "At the crank of the windlass in the well," "Salt," "If I could just one syphon off," and "The Earth's Rind" are reprinted here by the kind permission of the author. Translation copyright © 2002 Jamie McKendrick.

ALLEN MANDELBAUM. "Ancient one, I am drunk with the call," "At times – suddenly – ," "I should have liked to fell harsh and essential," and "In sleep" first appeared in *Pequod* (Winter 1977), in a special Montale issue edited by Jonathan Galassi, and were revised for the UK edition of this collection. They are reprinted here by the kind permission of the author. Translation copyright © 1977 and 2002 Allen Mandelbaum.

JAMES MERRILL. "The House of the Customs Men" © 1952 by the Literary Estate of James Merrill. Reprinted with the permission of the Wylie Agency, Inc. "New Stanzas" © 1956 by the Literary Estate of James Merrill. Reprinted with the permission of the Wylie Agency, Inc. "The Eel" © 1952 by the Literary Estate of James Merrill. Reprinted with the permission of the Wylie Agency, Inc.

EDWIN MORGAN. "Sarcophagi I," "Dozing at midday, dazed and pale," "Bring me the sunflower to transplant here," "Peeweet,"

"Arsenio," "Lindau," "Low Tide," "New Stanzas," "The Eel," "Brief Testament," translated by Edwin Morgan, are reprinted from his book, *Collected Translations* (1996), by permission of Carcanet Press, Ltd. Translation copyright © 1996 Edwin Morgan.

DESMOND O'GRADY. "Delta" is reprinted by the kind permission of the author. Translation copyright © 1965 Desmond O'Grady.

ARSHI PIPA. "Many years, and a harder one by the foreign... ," from *Montale and Dante* (University of Minnesota Press, 1968). Reprinted by permission of the publishers. Translation copyright © 1968 Arshi Pipa.

MARIO PRAZ. "Arsenio." Translation copyright © 1928 Mario Praz.

SAMUEL PUTNAM. "Cuttle Bones," originally appeared in *This Quarter* (April, May, June 1930). Reprinted with permission of Hilary Putnam. Translation copyright © 1930 Hilary Putnam.

SONIA RAIZISS. "Maybe some morning, walking in dry glass air" is reprinted by the kind permission of Alfredo de Palchi. Translation copyright © 1962 Alfredo de Palchi and the Estate of Sonia Raiziss. "On the Scrawled Wall" appeared first in *Poetry* (May 1958). Translation copyright © 1958 the Estate of Sonia Raiziss.

JEREMY REED. All translations are from *The Coastguard's House* (Bloodaxe Books, 1990). Reprinted by permission of PFD on behalf of Jeremy Reed. Translation copyright © 1990 Jeremy Reed.

VINIO ROSSI. "You gave my name to a tree? That's not much;" first appeared in *Field: Contemporary Poetry and Politics*, no. 23, Fall 1980. © Oberlin College Press. It is part two of "Three Private Madrigals," translated by David Young and Vinio Rossi. It appears here by the kind permission of David Young. Translation copyright © 1980 Vinio Rossi and David Young.

DONALD SHEEHAN. "Afloat" and "In a Void" first appeared in *Satura: Five Poems by Eugenio Montale* (1969). They are reprinted here by the kind permission of David Keller and Donald Sheehan. Translation copyright © 1969 David Keller and Donald Sheehan.

G. SINGH. "Late in the Night" and "The Carillon Pendulum Clock," by Eugenio Montale, translated by G. Singh, from *New Poems*, copyright © 1990, 1972 by Eugenio Montale and G. Singh. Reprinted by permission of New Directions Publishing Corp.

BERNARD SPENCER. "The Lemon Trees" and "Bring me the sunflower" copyright © Mrs. Anne Humphreys, 1981. Reprinted from Bernard Spencer: *Collected Poems,* edited by Roger Bowen (1981), by permission Oxford University Press.

HARRY THOMAS. "To pass the noon, intent and pale" and "Sorapis, 40 Years Ago" are reprinted from volume 2, number 3 of *Literary Imagination: The Review of the Association of Literary Scholars and Critics,* copyright © 2000. Used by permission of the ALSC. "To pass the noon, intent and pale," "Xenia I," "Xenia II," and "Sorapis, 40 Years Ago," translation copyright © 2000 Harry Thomas.

N.S. THOMPSON. "Nixon in Rome" is reprinted here by the kind permission of the author. Translation copyright © 1981 N.S. Thompson.

BERNARD WALL. "Hitler Spring," translation copyright © 1949 the Estate of Bernard Wall. "The Wood Grouse" and "The Red and the Black," translation copyright © 1974 the Estate of Bernard Wall.

WILLIAM WEAVER. "House at the Sea" is reprinted here by the kind permission of the author. Translation copyright © William Weaver.

RACHEL WETZSTEON. "The violent thrum of error" and "Mistletoe, a city of snapshots," reprinted by permission from *Raritan: A Quarterly Review*, Vol. XIV, No. 2 (Fall 1994); "Blind Date," from *The Other Stars* by Rachel Wetzsteon, copyright © 1994 by Rachel Wetzsteon. These poems are reprinted here by the kind permission of the author.

CHARLES WRIGHT. "Tattoo 20: You stand in your shoes, two shiny graves," from *Bloodlines*, copyright © 1975 by Charles Wright and reprinted by permission of Wesleyan University Press; "Where the Tennis Court Was," "Beach at Versilia," and "Anniversary," from *The Storm & Other Poems*, Eugenio Montale, translated by Charles Wright, FIELD Translation Series 1 (Oberlin, OH: Oberlin College, 1978). Reprinted by permission of Oberlin College Press.

DAVID YOUNG. "You gave my name to a tree? That's not much;" first appeared in *Field: Contemporary Poetry and Politics*, no. 23, Fall 1980. © Oberlin College Press. It is part two of "Three Private Madrigals," translated by David Young and Vinio Rossi. It appears here by the kind permission of David Young. Translation copyright © 1980 Vinio Rossi and David Young.

INDEX OF TRANSLATORS
AND POETS